Is Global Capitalism Working?

Foreign Affairs Readers

A New Europe? (1998)
The Rise of China (1998)
Is Global Capitalism Working? (1998)
Asia: Rising or Falling? (1998)
Democracy (1998)
Bosnia: What Went Wrong? (1998)

Foreign Affairs Agenda: The New Shape of World Politics (1997)
The Marshall Plan and Its Legacy (1997)
Clash of Civilizations: The Debate (1996)
Competitiveness: An International Economics Reader (1994)

For information, or to order Foreign Affairs Readers, visit www.foreignaffairs.org.

Is Global Capitalism Working?

Ethan B. Kapstein
Wolfgang H. Reinicke
Jessica T. Mathews
Anne-Marie Slaughter
Peter F. Drucker
Robert O. Keohane *and* Joseph S. Nye, Jr.
Martin Feldstein
Stanley Fischer
Jagdish Bhagwati
Richard Haass *and* Robert Litan

A FOREIGN AFFAIRS READER

Printed in the United States of America.

For information on Foreign Affairs *Readers, visit www.foreignaffairs.org or email ForAff@cfr.org.*

A FOREIGN AFFAIRS READER

ISBN: 0-87609-238-5

CONTENTS

Introduction

Foreign Affairs *Readers bring together important essays first published in* Foreign Affairs. *We include a variety of articles, serving different purposes. Some may be pieces of reportage, others may strongly argue a specific point of view, still others may be statesmen's memoirs.*

Each volume presents a structured, focused set of our best essays on a specific topic. Both the topic and the essays have been chosen with a particular purpose in mind – classroom use. Most of the essays advance a thesis or provide important information that is likely to stimulate students to think and discuss the broader subject. Some are current, others were written a while ago. The latter are included because the arguments they advance are still crucial to understanding the issues. We exclude many articles, which, while excellent in other respects, might not contribute as much to discussion in the classroom.

For over 75 years, Foreign Affairs *has prided itself on publishing only the very best analytic writing on political, economic, and social trends around the globe. We hope that this collection succeeds in linking scholarship and the reality of today's world.*

A complete listing of Foreign Affairs *Readers appears at the front of this volume.*

Workers and the World Economy

Ethan B. Kapstein

BREAKING THE POSTWAR BARGAIN

THE GLOBAL economy is leaving millions of disaffected workers in its train. Inequality, unemployment, and endemic poverty have become its handmaidens. Rapid technological change and heightening international competition are fraying the job markets of the major industrialized countries. At the same time systemic pressures are curtailing every government's ability to respond with new spending. Just when working people most need the nation-state as a buffer from the world economy, it is abandoning them.

This is not how things were supposed to work. The failure of today's advanced global capitalism to keep spreading the wealth poses a challenge not just to policymakers but to modern economic "science" as well. For generations, students were taught that increasing trade and investment, coupled with technological change, would drive national productivity and create wealth. Yet over the past decade, despite a continuing boom in international trade and finance, productivity has faltered, and inequality in the United States and unemployment in Europe have worsened.

President Bill Clinton may have been right to proclaim that "the era of big government is over," and perhaps the American people will ultimately decide that those who need assistance should look elsewhere for help. But if the post–World War II social contract with workers—of full

---

ETHAN B. KAPSTEIN is Director of Studies at the Council on Foreign Relations. His most recent book is *Governing the Global Economy: International Finance and the State.*

employment and comprehensive social welfare—is to be broken, political support for the burgeoning global economy could easily collapse. For international economic integration is not some uncontrollable fact of life, but has deepened because of a series of policy decisions taken by the major industrial powers over the last 45 years. It is time to recognize that those decisions, while benefiting the world economy as a whole, have begun to have widespread negative consequences. The forces acting on today's workers inhere in the structure of today's global economy, with its open and increasingly fierce competition on the one hand and fiscally conservative units—states—on the other. Countermeasures, therefore, must also be deep, sustained, and widespread. Easing pressures on the "losers" of the new open economy must now be the focus of economic policy if the process of globalization is to be sustained.

It is hardly sensationalist to claim that in the absence of broad-based policies and programs designed to help working people, the political debate in the United States and many other countries will soon turn sour. Populists and demagogues of various stripes will find "solutions" to contemporary economic problems in protectionism and xenophobia. Indeed, in every industrialized nation, such figures are on the campaign trail. Growing income inequality, job insecurity, and unemployment are widely seen as the flip side of globalization. That perception must be changed if Western leaders wish to maintain the international system their predecessors created. After all, the fate of the global economy ultimately rests on domestic politics in its constituent states.

The spread of the dogma of restrictive fiscal policy is undermining the bargain struck with workers in every industrial country. States are basically telling their workers that they can no longer afford the postwar deal and must minimize their obligations. The current obsession with balanced budgets in the United States and the Maastricht criteria in Europe must be replaced by an equally vigilant focus on growth and equity. National responses to this global problem are likely to fail, as any state that deviates from "responsible" economic policies will be punished by currency markets and bondholders. States must now reorient their economic policies toward growth, but it should be done as part of a coordinated international effort. Calling for such economic policy coordination might seem utopian in the current political environment, but it has been done before.

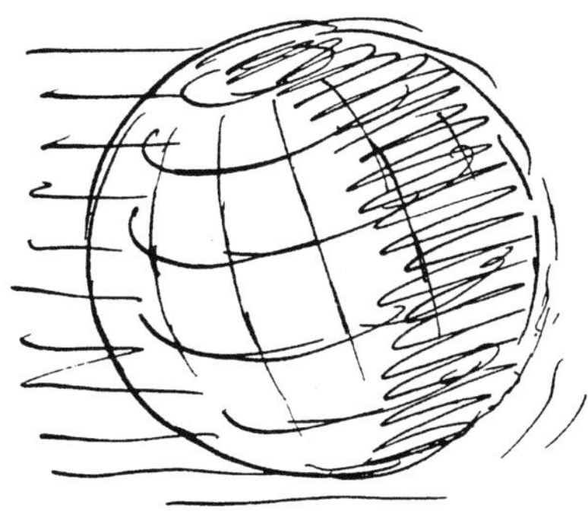

The world may be moving inexorably toward one of those tragic moments that will lead future historians to ask, why was nothing done in time? Were the economic and policy elites unaware of the profound disruption that economic and technological change were causing working men and women? What prevented them from taking the steps necessary to prevent a global social crisis?

THE GREAT TRANSFORMATION

THE CURRENT predicament is hardly unprecedented. Writing in *Progress and Poverty* in 1879, the reformer Henry George observed that "at the beginning of this marvelous era it was natural to expect, and it was expected, that laborsaving inventions would lighten the toil and improve the condition of the laborer; that the enormous increase in the power of producing wealth would make real poverty a thing of the past." George chronicled the many technologies, such as the steam engine and telegraph, that had been introduced in his lifetime, and the great explosion in commerce and trade that followed.

But far from heralding an era of prosperity, "disappointment has followed disappointment. From all parts of the civilized world come complaints of industrial depression . . . of want and suffering and anxiety among the working classes." George observed that the massive investment in technology had only resulted in increasing returns to capital and falling wages for working people. Thus "the mere laborer has no more interest in the general advance of productive power than the Cuban slave has . . . in the price of sugar."

During the nineteenth century, the world enjoyed a secular increase in trade and investment under the aegis of a liberal Great Britain, while the adoption of the international gold standard created the illusion of domestic financial stability. But profound social dislocation accompanied this process of globalization and would eventually contribute to its undoing.

Britain's decision in 1846 to lift the Corn Laws, which had long protected domestic agriculture, is the classic example of a policy consciously designed to globalize the economy in favor of specific interests. With industrialization, the Manchester factory owners needed more labor. The simple solution was to get farm hands off the land and pay them low wages. The most efficient way to achieve this goal was to introduce foreign competition in agricultural products, forcing down prices and ensuring that farmers and tenants could no longer earn their livelihood. Labor flooded into the cities, and these workers were paid relatively low wages because the price of food—their major expenditure—was falling.

Throughout the Industrial Revolution various regulations that had long governed economic life—many dating back to the Middle Ages—were dismantled, and rural laborers found their traditional ways of life torn asunder. Workers became commodities like grain and coal, with demand for and supply of their services a function of market requirements. Such a laissez-faire approach to labor markets was inherently unstable, as the philosopher Karl Polanyi later explained in *The Great Transformation.* He described the process by which landless working people throughout Europe entered a world of urban poverty, creating a political cauldron. During periods of prolonged depression these laborers became easy prey for extremist political forces. Polanyi argued that it was the complete unraveling of economic and labor market regulations and traditions in the nineteenth

century that caused such tremendous social and political upheaval in the early twentieth, culminating in the collapse of the world economy and the outbreak of the First and Second World Wars.

The Great Transformation was published in 1944, the year that the Bretton Woods conference to restructure the international economy was held. And it was Polanyi's version of history that the postwar policymakers brought with them. As Treasury Secretary Henry Morgenthau said, "All of us have seen the great economic tragedy of our time. We saw the worldwide depression of the 1930s. We saw currency disorders develop and spread from land to land, destroying the basis for international trade and international investment and even international faith. In their wake, we saw unemployment and wretchedness. . . . We saw their victims fall prey . . . to demagogues and dictators. We saw bewilderment and bitterness become the breeders of fascism, and finally, of war." The post–World War II global economy resulted from a series of conscious policy decisions, reached in the belief that increased economic exchange could be a force for world peace and prosperity.

The postwar leaders were committed to rebuilding the world economy, but this time with a significant difference. In globalization's previous incarnation, governments had done little to protect working people from its malign effects, and their mistake exacted a price in revolutions and war. Having learned from that experience, statesmen now designed a liberal world economy that maintained an active domestic role for the state in order to ensure that equity and growth went hand in hand.

Thus the new global economy would include both domestic and international components. Of greatest significance, the state would supervise most aspects of economic life. In the United States, for example, the Truman administration passed the Employment Act, which set as its objective full employment, and the G.I. Bill, which provided veterans with education and housing benefits. Across Europe, ambitious social welfare policies were enacted. In every industrial country, labor was not to be treated as a commodity, subject to the free market's destructive whims, and the organization of workers into labor unions was actively encouraged. The implicit agreement struck between states and their societies—what John G. Ruggie has termed the bargain of "embedded liberalism"—ensured that the gains from economic globalization would be used to compensate the losers in the interests of political stability.[1]

Western leaders constructed international regimes for money and trade that by charter were to be responsive to domestic political and economic concerns. When they launched the General Agreement on Tariffs and Trade (GATT) to liberalize and expand commerce among the member states, they also established safeguards to protect workers from unfair trade practices and to assist those who were displaced. When they created an international monetary system to avoid ceaseless rounds of competitive currency devaluation, they also established the International Monetary Fund (IMF) as a lender of last resort for balance-of-payments emergencies. When they formed a European Common Market to promote regional trade and investment, they also permitted states to retain considerable autonomy in social policy.

But the Bretton Woods order would prove unsustainable. It was very generous to workers and capitalists, but it required high levels of economic growth. The oil crises of 1973-74 and 1978-79 hammered the industrial countries, prompting stagflation, that insidious mixture of stagnation and inflation. Furthermore, increasing foreign trade meant greater competition for national firms, while financial deregulation permitted capital to become more footloose. These developments, in turn, led to widespread corporate restructuring and a glut of unskilled labor, which translated into higher unemployment, less tax revenue, and greater pressure on state resources. The crisis of the welfare state had begun.

Faced with the exploding costs of cradle-to-grave support for increasingly idle populations, Western states in the 1980s began to adopt stringent monetary and fiscal policies. Workers, of course, have had little say in this process. Indeed, what governments are really trying to do is break their postwar deal with workers while maintaining their commitment to an open economy. They cannot have it both ways, and instead the policy focus should be on negotiating a package that helps workers adjust to ongoing economic changes.

---

[1]John G. Ruggie, "International Regimes, Transactions, and Change: Embedded Liberalism in the Postwar Economic Order," *International Organization*, Spring 1982, pp. 195-231.

Ethan B. Kapstein

WORKERS OF THE WORLD

NOBODY DISPUTES that the past two decades have been cruel to unskilled workers in the industrial countries. Growing income inequality has given rise to millions of working poor in the United States, and this sorry condition is now becoming apparent in Western Europe. Between 1973 and 1993 the real hourly wage of Americans without a high school diploma fell from $11.85 an hour to $8.64 an hour. In the early 1970s households in the top 5 percent of the income bracket earned 10 times more than those in the bottom 5 percent; today they make almost 15 times more. Similar trends are evident in Britain and even that most egalitarian country, Sweden.

Workers have been further squeezed by the decline in manufacturing employment. Manufacturing employment in the United States fell by 1.4 million between 1978 and 1990. Those who lost their jobs were, in general, the unskilled, and when they found new work it was usually at lower pay. The experience has now become familiar to middle managers as well, as evidenced by the recent spate of major corporate layoffs. The failure of the industrial sector to generate new jobs has been a major cause of labor's economic problems, and perhaps some of America's social problems more generally. Fully two percent of all working-age American men are behind bars.

In Western Europe, the unemployment figures are frightening. In France, average unemployment between 1969 and 1973 was 2.6 percent; today it is over 11 percent. In Germany the rate was below 1 percent; today it is approaching 10 percent. In Belgium, the unemployment rate has quadrupled over the past 20 years. The Europeans have created a lost generation of workers and are now suffering for it in terms of increased crime, drug abuse, violence against immigrants, and the increasing popularity of extremist political groups. In this context, it is sobering to realize that Germany's current level of four million unemployed is the highest it has been since the early 1930s.

At the same time, there has been a dramatic decline in unionized labor in both the United States and Europe. The unionized portion of the U.S. labor force has dropped by more than one-third—from 25 to 16 percent—since the 1970s, and organized labor is also declining in Austria, France, Germany, Italy, the Netherlands, Switzerland,

and the United Kingdom.[2] Labor is losing its political voice, and the consequences of its demise—lower wages and benefits for unskilled workers, greater job insecurity, and less political interest in the economic losers—should not be dismissed.

Further, it should be recalled that organized labor in the north has been a prime mover behind unionization and the promotion of human rights in the developing countries of the south. International activism by unions has been a help to workers in Latin America and other countries struggling to win the right to collective bargaining, as well as better health and safety standards. Now that all industrial workers—unionized or not—could benefit from this type of activism in such countries as China and India, and other non- or anti-union regions of the world, organized labor is no longer vigorous enough to play this role. To be sure, unions are hardly perfect; they too form entrenched interests that hinder labor market flexibility and job creation. But their historical role in economic development and social equity has been forgotten.

THE BATTLE OF THE CAUSES

SOLUTIONS TO these bleak trends need not await some consensus among economists about their causes. Policymakers debating these issues are like firefighters idly wondering what started the blaze while the house burns to the ground. The two traditional culprits that have once again emerged from the economics literature are trade and technology. A third, cited by few economists but by some journalists and politicians, is immigration.

Economists who focus on the effects of trade, such as Adrian Wood, have argued that the contemporary problems of unskilled workers in the north are linked to a strong increase in trade between north and south and a change in its composition.[3] Historically, the developing countries provided the industrial world with agricultural goods and raw materials in exchange for manufactured goods. The

[2]Melvin Reder and Lloyd Ulman, "Unionism and Unification," in *Labor and an Integrated Europe,* ed. Lloyd Ulman, Barry Eichengreen, and William T. Dickens, Washington: The Brookings Institution, 1993, p. 24.

[3]Adrian Wood, *North-South Trade, Employment and Inequality: Changing Futures in a Skill-driven World,* New York: Oxford University Press, 1994.

gains from such trade have been analyzed and extolled by economists since David Ricardo, sustaining the free trade movement.

Such trade is rightly celebrated, since it makes nations wealthier than they would otherwise be. More recently, however, the south has moved into the business of manufacturing, from clothing to consumer electronics. Today such goods account for over 50 percent of the south's exports and surpass its commodity exports in value. As is well known, workers in these developing countries are generally paid peanuts for their labor—less than a dollar an hour in such countries as China, India, and Pakistan—and in many countries, including China, they are prevented by law from forming unions or otherwise bargaining collectively.

According to a theory proposed by Paul A. Samuelson and Wolfgang Stolper in 1941, two countries that practice free trade and have the same technology should eventually see their wages equalize. In effect, wages in the First World are forced down by competition from developing countries in similar industries. Ironically, even though falling wages would seem to confirm Stolper-Samuelson, some economists are now claiming that its assumptions are wrong.[4]

In Western Europe wages are less skewed than in the United States, but the continent has paid for relative equality with higher unemployment. Economic theory also helps to explain why this is so. If Germany begins importing Polish goods produced with unskilled labor, and regulations and other rigidities prevent wages from falling to Polish levels, unemployment among unskilled German workers will rise in the absence of new job creation.

Many American economists, such as Paul Krugman and Robert Z. Lawrence, contest these explanations. They point out that foreign trade remains too small a share of economic activity in most industrial nations to be responsible for such large and pervasive phenomena as unemployment and income inequality, and they assert that technology must be responsible for these changes. According to this school of thought, the introduction of new technology—say, computers—creates a surplus of unskilled labor. At the same time, the new technology

---

[4]See, for instance, Jagdish Bhagwati and Vivek H. Dehejia, "Freer Trade and Wages of the Unskilled—Is Marx Striking Again?" in *Trade and Wages: Leveling Wages Down?* ed. Jagdish Bhagwati and Marvin H. Kosters, Washington: AEI Press, 1994, pp. 36-75.

increases the demand for the skilled workers who know how to run it, raising their wages. As a result, income inequality widens because of the good old-fashioned law of supply and demand. The evidence for this line of reasoning is the heavy investment in new technology by manufacturing during the 1980s, when growing wage inequality became apparent in the United States.

But economists are wrong to treat trade and technology as competing explanations. A significant share of new technology, for example, has been induced by foreign competition. Indeed, when one looks at those industries that have suffered great job losses on the one hand and enjoyed significant investment in new technology on the other, they are concentrated in sectors, like steel and automobiles, that have faced tremendous pressure from imports. Still, the widespread introduction of technology across many sectors suggests that domestic competition spurred much of this investment.

As a general explanation, technology is unsatisfactory. It is never clearly distinguished from other kinds of capital, and there is no reason that its introduction must in principle reduce the wages of the unskilled. Technology is for economists the residual that accounts for everything their theories cannot.

Yet a final explanation for labor's lament is immigration. During the 1980s the United States had the largest immigration boom in its postwar history. Between 1980 and 1989 more than six million legal immigrants alone came to its shores. In 1994 more than three million arrived illegally. The net effect of legal migration has been positive. The new arrivals bring needed skills, create businesses and jobs, and raise output. At the same time, the pool of unskilled labor has also increased, forcing down their wages. As with other facets of globalization, increased migration benefits countries overall, but it hurts some groups. The failure to address their dislocation will allow nativists to seize the debate, creating a more permissive environment not only for protectionism but for hate crimes, as is already evident in Western Europe.

RETRAINING REDUX

WHICHEVER EXPLANATION is most important, the fact remains that technological change, free trade, migration, and other forces such as defense cuts create losers as well as winners. The rationale for open economies is that, in principle, the gains will outweigh the losses for the country as a whole; thus, the winners can afford to compensate the losers. Under GATT and Bretton Woods, this compensation took the form of such short-term measures as trade adjustment programs, which provide unemployment insurance, retraining, and even support for moving to new communities. When a robust economy was creating lots of good jobs, everyone was made better off. But that is no longer the case. Today, a worker who loses his job is likely to find a new one only at lower pay. Indeed, as *The New York Times* reported earlier this year, 65 percent of workers who ultimately find jobs after a layoff do so only at lower levels of pay, and Morris Kleiner of the University of Minnesota has found that most such workers are still earning much less even five years later.

According to an analysis of dislocated defense workers in New England, defense workers should have an easy time finding new jobs, given their skills and experience with computers, precision tools, and quality control—even if these attributes have not been tested in the context of more highly competitive enterprises. But even among these workers, one in five of those who found new jobs had wage rates that "represented a pay cut of 40 percent or more." Indeed, over 60 percent of all dislocated workers "had noticeably lower hourly earnings."[5]

[5]Yolanda K. Kodrzycki, "The Costs of Defense-Related Layoffs in New England," *New England Economic Review*, March/April 1995, p. 16.

Their experience with retraining should also counsel caution. Some could not afford the costs associated with these programs, while others had difficulty matching training opportunities to projected new job requirements. For still others, the lack of growth prospects in even distantly related industries raised questions about whether retraining was really a good investment. Overall, as the World Bank's 1995 *World Development Report* concluded, results are mixed regarding the value of training in helping unemployed workers find new jobs.

But even if training is a good investment, the cost of providing it to all unemployed workers is prohibitive. There are now some 34 million unemployed persons in the member countries of the Organization for Economic Cooperation and Development (OECD). If the average cost of retraining for each worker is $7,000, the total bill would be $238 billion. For the United States, with its 7 million unemployed, the total would be $49 billion. Today, the U.S. government spends about $10 billion on work-related education and training. In the current fiscal environment, it is difficult to imagine that number rising by the required amount.

Policymakers debating causes are like firefighters letting the house burn down.

On the contrary, these programs are being cut back. Since 1992, funds for labor market training and other active measures have fallen in such countries as Canada, Germany, Sweden, and the United States, the last especially ironic since Secretary of Labor Robert Reich is one of training's greatest devotees (though in fairness, he does have to contend with a Republican Congress). Incredibly, public spending for higher education has also fallen. In the United States, such expenditures were cut 10 percent in the early 1990s, and in Britain only marginally less. At the same time, in countries with federal structures, where the constituent states were expected to assume increased public burdens, local crises and fiscal stringency prevented them from taking up the slack. This is the very problem facing many Russian regions and American states.

It is odd that training has become the mom and apple pie of economists and public officials across the political spectrum when it could at best provide only a partial answer to the problems of dislocated workers, at least given the knowledge base about what works at current spending levels. Indeed, one learns in economics that policymakers should choose the most direct and efficient means for solving problems. This lesson suggests that if the concern is income inequality, policies should be adopted to close the income gap. If the concern is unemployment, more jobs should be created. Training should not be abandoned, of course, but it is not by itself a solution.

KEEPING GROWTH DOWN

IN DEVELOPING positive solutions, however, it is important to recognize that declining rates of economic growth, caused largely by a drop-off in productivity, are hurting all workers. Curiously, analysts have paid less attention to these indexes than to unemployment and inequality. But had the industrial countries continued to grow in the 1990s at their earlier postwar rates, many current headline issues would hardly attract attention. If growth had remained at the 1960s average of 3.5 percent instead of current levels of just over 2 percent, more jobs of all kinds would have been created, rectifying unemployment in Europe and obviating inequality in the United States.

In truth, this productivity slowdown remains a puzzle. Why is it happening if the industrial countries have invested heavily in technology and opened their economies to foreign competition? These things should have spurred productivity growth. At present there is no good answer, though hypotheses focus on such diverse factors as the widespread shift from manufacturing to services in the north, and the decline in educational attainment, especially in science and math, among workers in many of the industrial countries.

Between 1971 and 1978, according to the OECD, the members of the Group of Seven (G-7) enjoyed an average economic growth rate of 3.5 percent per year, and this during a period of severe oil shocks, with the consequent rise in energy prices and inflation. Since 1989, by contrast, growth has averaged 2.1 percent. For Japan, the drop has been even steeper. Its average growth between 1971 and 1978 was 4.5 percent, a number that has fallen in the 1990s to 2.4 percent. Meanwhile, between 1979 and 1994, unemployment in the OECD rose from 17.7 million and a rate of 5.1 percent to 34 million and a rate of 8 percent.

Unfortunately, this slowdown in the 1990s followed on the heels of a period of inflation, deficit spending, and increasing government debt levels around the industrial world. In the G-7 the interest payments on government debt rose from 1.6 percent of GDP in 1980 to 2.5 percent in 1990. Today the figure stands at 2.8 percent. In order to stabilize their financial affairs, states adopted stringent monetary and, more recently, fiscal policies—in short, policies deemed sustainable or credible by financial markets. These policies privileged financial stability over employment. They were the welfare state's equivalent of a grapefruit diet. The problem is that, as with all diets, they can become obsessive and cause more harm than good.

Over time, special interest groups have become entrenched around particular sets of policies, creating bureaucratic sclerosis. Restrictive economic policies—reduced deficits, reduced spending, reduced taxes, and the most exalted deity, low inflation—have favored financial interests at the expense of workers and have created an international rentier class. For anyone with money to invest, the last 20 years have been bountiful. Fiscally restrictive policies have become an ideology of this class for all practical purposes, defended in the pages of the leading newspapers and economic journals and most of the Beltway think tanks. Public officials who adopt restrictive measures are labeled "responsible" by editorialists, and the markets reward their behavior, sustaining the ideology.

The politics of financial credibility has played out somewhat differently across the industrial world. In the United States they have centered around the balanced budget debate between President Clinton and Congress. Indeed, they led to Clinton's Hoover-like statement about big government in his recent State of the Union address. Policies have targeted inflation and fiscal expansion in recent years, but the benefits of this approach have yet to be widely shared. At the same time, polling data and other evidence, such as the results of the Republican presidential primaries, suggest that the American people are becoming increasingly worried about their economic security and want the government to do something about it. And this concern is not solely a local phenomenon. What in America was once called the battle between Wall Street and Main Street has now become global.

The budget debate is a case of ideology overriding economics. In fact, there is no reason a balanced budget must always be favored over

Keynesian deficit spending. As economist Robert Eisner wrote in *How Real Is the Federal Deficit?* in 1986, "Deficits can be too small as well as too large." He reminds us that when "there is slack in the economy, deficit-induced demand stimulates output and employment." It may well be the case that Clinton has gone too far in agreeing with congressional Republicans about the need to balance the budget over the next seven years.

But there is no direct correlation between deficit spending and inflation, as Japan demonstrates. During most of the postwar era Japan has had far higher deficits than the United States as a percentage of GNP, but lower inflation. The reason is Japan's credibility when it comes to maintaining monetary stability. Given Japan's high savings rate, the markets have confidence in its ability to finance long-term debt obligations. Today Japan is the only industrial country that is taking a Keynesian approach to its economic problems, and its latest growth figures suggest that fiscal expansion has been beneficial. There is, in short, no reason that moderate fiscal relaxation must generate high inflation. Moreover, to the extent that Japanese levels of inflation become somewhat higher than those in the United States, they would contribute to easing tensions over the yen-dollar exchange rate.

In contrast, leaders in Europe, where deficits are also higher than in the United States, have demanded a rapid reduction in government spending in order to meet the criteria of the Maastricht treaty on monetary union. With Germany setting the economic rules of the game according to its domestic preferences, European states that wish to participate in the planned union must reduce their budget deficits to 3 percent of GDP by 1999. In France, where deficits are now running at 5 percent of GDP, the rules mean applying the ax to the state budget. These policies reflect an obsessive fear of Europe's traditional bouts of inflation, but the major central banks have done a credible job of maintaining monetary stability. What has been the point of adopting these anti-inflationary policies if they do not permit governments some fiscal room to maneuver?

Even in Russia one can see restrictive fiscal policies dismantling earlier contracts between the state and society. Thus, under stringent IMF discipline, Russia too must reduce its budget deficit. Those hardest hit have been pensioners, the unemployed, and the poor—again, the people most in need of state services. The collapse of the social safety net in Russia explains why the Communist Party received the largest share of the vote in the December 1995 Duma elections and why its leader, Gennadi Zyuganov, may be elected the country's president in June 1996.

LOOSENING UP

TO MEET THE growing problems of working people, governments must develop a coherent package of economic policies and programs supported by international policy coordination that generates renewed growth. Such a strategy, which will require some fiscal relaxation, has some costs, but the consequences of doing nothing will be worse, since disastrous measures like protectionism and nativism are again being mentioned, even in economically literate circles.

The starting point for any policy effort of this kind is the normative assertion that the appropriate goal of economic policy is to improve the lives of the citizenry. Monetary and fiscal policies should be structured in such a way as to ensure the fundamental promise that working people can earn a living wage. This means that in every industrial country policies must be directed toward helping people cope with the consequences of economic change. Of course, the appropriate policy mix will vary. In the United States, job insecurity, income inequality, and the plight of the working poor are now chief concerns. In Europe, job creation is key. Thus the policy for Europe would permit greater fiscal relaxation and that for the United States more income redistribution.

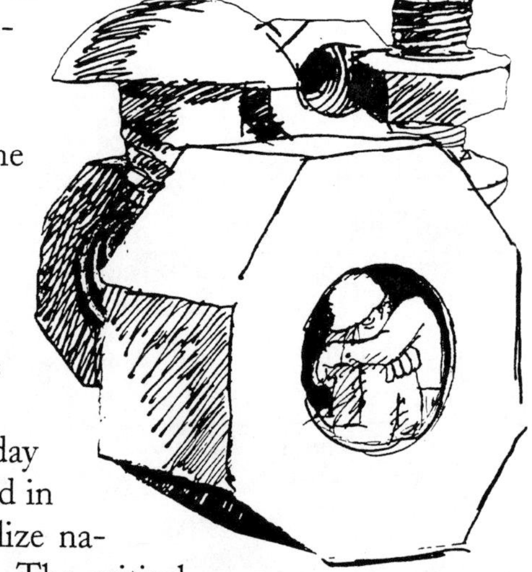

The argument that present-day fiscal restrictions must be maintained in order to balance budgets and stabilize national economies is without merit. The critical issue on the fiscal side is how governments spend the money. Just as with corporate investment, there is a difference between investments that are likely to yield long-term benefits and those that throw money down rat holes. To take an extreme case, no American during World War II said that the investment in armaments was a bad one, and it was gladly financed through bond issues and payroll taxes. Contemporary critics who would say that spending money on labor policies is unfair to the nation's children forget that the best thing that can be bequeathed to the next generation is social peace.

There is no direct correlation between deficit spending and inflation.

An expansionary strategy must include both microeconomic and macroeconomic elements, coupled with international policy coordination. Microeconomic policies, like the expansion of education and training, are needed to provide workers with the skills that will enable them to rejoin the labor market or find better career prospects. But these policies and programs are of little value if the economy is not producing good jobs. Macroeconomic policies, like fiscal relaxation and changes in taxation, are therefore required to provide a stimulus to spur economic growth. Taken together, these micro- and macroeconomic policies should translate into a better-educated and more productive work force. Finally, international policy coordination is necessary so that countries can develop expansionary policies within a collective framework, avoiding competitive currency depreciations that in the long run hurt everyone.

Governments that wish to assist unskilled workers have four choices: protectionism, education and training, public works programs and employment subsidies, and tax policy and income transfers. All of them entail costs, which must be paid for in one way or another.

Protectionism has received both renewed attention and scrutiny since candidate Patrick Buchanan's victory in the New Hampshire presidential primary. Buchanan, an avowed "economic nationalist," would place prohibitive tariffs on a range of imports in order to protect American jobs and wages. Unfortunately, whatever the alleged benefits of protectionism, the costs would outweigh them for most workers, and national income would certainly fall. Protectionism would lead to higher prices for all products, both foreign and domestic, resulting in lower consumption and an economic slowdown. Furthermore, America's trading partners could not be expected to sit passively while they were victimized; they too would erect higher trade barriers in response, eliminating markets for U.S. exports and the high-wage jobs that go with them. Since exports are the fastest-growing segment of the economy, policies that lead to their restriction deserve condemnation. In short, protectionism is a remedy that is worse than the disease.

Increased spending on education and training appears to be the only policy intervention that meets with universal approval across the political spectrum. Over a generation, unskilled workers will respond to the economic signals and opt for more education and training. Historical evidence suggests that this process occurs in most industrial countries undergoing significant economic change.[6] But the benefits of training for dislocated workers are uncertain, and the costs of universal training would be prohibitive. Clearly, the expansion of educational opportunities should play a central role in any democratic society and should be financed—it makes for good politics and good economics. It cannot, however, provide anything resembling a near-term solution to the structural problems of unemployment and inequality.

The third approach is to increase the number of jobs through public works programs or, perhaps more effectively, employment subsidies to the private sector. Few Western countries have pursued this tack as an explicit policy since the Great Depression, but it should be remembered that the New Deal was successful in creating jobs and reducing misery. Public job creation is relatively efficient and socially productive—since it provides younger workers with needed job experience—and it can be done fairly quickly. If the government subsidizes jobs, it will get more of them. Such policies, however, must be designed carefully to avoid an unproductive substitution of subsidized for unsubsidized workers.

This approach becomes all the more compelling in light of the sharp defense drawdowns among the member states of NATO. In the United States, for example, the size of the military force has shrunk

[6] Jeffrey G. Williamson, *Inequality, Poverty, and History*, Cambridge: Blackwell, 1991.

by nearly one million since 1986, closing a once-promising route to education, training, experience, and responsibility for thousands of young adults. France will soon end military conscription. Alternative paths must be forged to help this population enter the workforce. Moreover, public works spending would counteract the fiscal drag of these defense cuts.

Finally, it is clear that tax policy and income transfers must play a key role in any serious effort to help working people and to finance new programs. One possible approach, combining in a sense the best of candidate Steve Forbes' flat tax and Senator Jeff Bingaman's (D-N.M.) proposal to tax financial transactions, would be to lower overall federal income tax rates—perhaps eliminating income taxes altogether for a large number of the working poor—while making them sharply more progressive up the income ladder. In the United States, the fiscal gap that resulted could then be covered by introducing a national value-added tax, at least on luxury goods. Most industrial countries already have a VAT. In principle, workers would still pay less in overall taxes, since their VAT payments would be lower than their income taxes under the current system, while the rich, who now enjoy a variety of tax loopholes, could not escape paying their fair share of the VAT. Most important, more job-related services could be provided than is now the case.

Public job creation is relatively efficient and socially productive.

In Europe, unemployment rather than income distribution is the key problem. Additional reforms are needed there if the goal is to increase labor market flexibility, the hiring of new workers, and small business creation. Again, the policies are not a mystery, and inaction reflects a lack of political will rather than of economic knowledge. Among these reforms, reductions in employer social charges such as health care costs and greater flexibility in hiring, firing, and setting work hours are absolute necessities. Small and medium-sized enterprises in particular, which are important generators of new jobs, are being stymied by these onerous charges. Furthermore, unemployment and other benefits in most European countries are simply out of proportion, and they give the jobless little incentive to seek work. Here, the Europeans probably could learn something from the United

States. Savings in these areas could provide funds for programs that create employment. Unfortunately, Europe's technocratic leaders have done a poor job of explaining the economic situation to voters and have lacked imagination in promoting new ideas.

A recent Brookings Institution study of the policies needed to restore growth in the U.S. economy, including funds for education and training and adding spending for research and development, estimates annual expenditures on the order of $80 billion, a large but not Himalayan sum. In Europe with its far higher levels of unemployment, the costs would likely be greater. To pay for this program, the authors call for higher taxes on upper income groups, coupled with spending cuts in other areas, presumably defense. While one can disagree with the specifics, the cost estimate suggests the magnitude of the task that confronts decision-makers.

One of the main arguments against an expansionary strategy, of course, is that it is inflationary. In the current climate, inflation can be avoided if monetary discipline is maintained. But in the event, some inflation overseas, as in the Japanese case, might well suit American interests. For Europe, it may be time to reassess the costs associated with the doctrinaire German approach to monetary policy. While inflation is a scourge, so is double-digit unemployment, with its dangers to the global economy.

HANGING TOGETHER

NO SINGLE formula would produce an optimal set of policy reforms. Each industrial country must find its own mix, given its particular political and economic circumstances. But these efforts will be more effective if pursued as part of an international effort. Without such policy coordination countries will either be penalized by financial markets for adopting growth-oriented policies or they will aggressively pursue beggar-thy-neighbor currency devaluations.

Effective coordination in the G-7 is not impossible; the global economy could not have been built without it. Nor is there a risk that such growth-oriented coordination would be undermined by massive capital flight to East Asia or other regions, since the United States and other Western countries still dominate the global financial marketplace. According to the OECD, in 1994 member countries were home to 90 percent of world stock market capitalization and bond issues.

A precedent for cooperation during hard times is the Bonn Summit of 1978. As the world economy was recovering from the oil crisis of 1973-74, the OECD called on governments to stimulate their economies to ensure that the growth prospects became a reality—remarkable in light of today's deflationary bias. The member countries agreed to a package of national measures that would collectively spur global growth. These included a reduction in U.S. oil imports, which led to a fall in world oil prices, and the implementation of expansionary policies in Germany and Japan. Unfortunately, the second oil crisis, caused by the Iranian Revolution, undercut most of these initiatives.

Like the Weimar elite, current leaders dismiss worker disaffection.

Why have Western countries eschewed this type of coordination in recent years? If they truly believe in globalization, they must accept that the economic performance of trading partners is converging. They should see such variables as growth rates, interest rates, and workers' wages approaching some common values. But instead, there are profound divergences in national economic performance, even in Western Europe, suggesting the continuing importance of domestic politics. This internecine competitiveness makes policy coordination difficult to achieve in the best of circumstances, but all the more so when growth is sluggish.

During the postwar decades, American leadership has time and again played a crucial role in leading the industrial countries out of the doldrums. The United States has assumed this burden not because it is magnanimous, but out of enlightened self-interest. Prosperous allies are needed for both economic and security reasons, and the OECD countries still generate by far the largest share of world trade. Today that leadership is absent. The president, perhaps pushed by Congress, seems to believe that domestic economic problems can be solved through domestic economic policies. The administration's singular focus on the international front has been export promotion. But American exports can increase only if the world economy continues to liberalize and grow.

This is an age of widespread economic insecurity, brought about by profound changes in trade, finance, and technology. For globalization to proceed, public officials in every country must give the lie to those who assert that it is anathema to workers' interests. The best way to make this case is by restoring growth and opportunity. Restrictive economic policies may have been necessary when first conceived in the 1980s to bring stability to financial markets, but they have failed too many people too long.

While the world stands at a critical time in postwar history, it has a group of leaders who appear unwilling, like their predecessors in the 1930s, to provide the international leadership to meet economic dislocations. Worse, many of them and their economic advisers do not seem to recognize the profound troubles affecting their societies. Like the German elite in Weimar, they dismiss mounting worker dissatisfaction, fringe political movements, and the plight of the unemployed and working poor as marginal concerns compared with the unquestioned importance of a sound currency and balanced budget. Leaders need to recognize the policy failures of the last 20 years and respond accordingly. If they do not, there are others waiting in the wings who will, perhaps on less pleasant terms.

Responses

Workers and Economists

The Global Economy Has Left Keynes in Its Train

First, Do No Harm

PAUL KRUGMAN

When a fire breaks out in a single-family home, firefighters know what they have to do. Fires in private houses are all pretty much alike. But when a fire breaks out in a warehouse, the firefighters make an effort to find out what is inside before they go to work, lest they do more harm than good. For example, if the warehouse is filled with highly flammable chemicals, dousing the building with water may spread the fire. In the end, the fire department must act regardless, but it is important to act on as much information as one can get about the nature of the problem.

I offer this homily because Ethan B. Kapstein uses an analogy with firefighting to claim that the West, faced with the economic difficulties of inequality and unemployment, has been paralyzed by too much debate over causes ("Workers and the World Economy," May/June 1996). He seems to believe that economic crises are like house fires, all pretty much the same. In particular, he seems to believe that the economic woes of advanced nations in the 1990s are basically similar to the problems of the 1930s. Deficit spending was the answer then and it is the answer now. Money should, therefore, be spent like water.

Economic crises, however, are not all the same, and the problems of the 1990s look very little like those of the 1930s. The good news is that while there is considerable dispute about the relative importance of some factors, economists have reached enough of a workable consensus about the nature of the problem to accommodate helpful policies. The bad news is that much, although not all, of what Kapstein has to say ignores this consensus, and that some of his policy recommendations are mischievous. They would either create the risk of renewed inflation and worsen the already shaky finances of Western governments, or they would contribute to the very policy paralysis Kapstein decries.

THE NOT-QUITE CONSENSUS

The economic difficulties of the advanced nations are not new. Unemployment in Europe has been rising steadily since the early 1970s, while inequality in the United States began rising sharply only a few

years later. Nor have they failed to receive attention. Over these 20-plus years, hundreds of conferences and thousands of academic articles and official reports have addressed them. While there is not a total consensus—there never is—a widely held middle-of-the-road position can be summarized by two propositions.

The first proposition is that the problems of wages and employment are mainly—forgive the jargon—structural rather than cyclical. A cyclical economic problem is caused by inadequate demand and can be cured by adopting a more expansionary monetary and fiscal policy—that is, spending more or taxing less. Structural economic problems cannot be solved in this way. Most economists now believe that the Great Depression was essentially cyclical; the slack in employment could have been taken up simply through an aggressive program of demand expansion. But the structural nature of Europe's unemployment was graphically demonstrated by the events of the late 1980s. The later stages of a broad business cycle recovery were marked by a noticeable increase in inflation (drastic in the case of the United Kingdom), despite the fact that the unemployment rate was still nearly nine percent. Demand had recovered, but unemployment could not fall below the nine-percent structural rate without triggering inflation.

What is wrong with trading off lower unemployment for slightly higher inflation? Not much, but that is the wrong question, because there is overwhelming evidence that inflation begets inflation. Suppose the Federal Reserve were to push the U.S. unemployment rate down from its current 5.5 percent to 4.5 percent. In the first year the inflation rate would probably rise only from its current 3 percent to 3.5 or 4 percent. But in the next year it would be 4 or 5 percent, the year after that 5 or 6 percent, and ever upward. The point, then, is not that inflation will explode if the unemployment rate is pushed too low. It is that a sustained effort to keep unemployment below the so-called NAIRU—the non-accelerating-inflation rate of unemployment—merely by stimulating demand will lead to an upward spiral of inflation. And though high rates of inflation would be slow to materialize, they would be equally hard to get rid of. Once the economy has developed six percent inflation, to get it back down to three percent would require a severe recession. Some countries have substantial room for demand expansion, most notably Japan. For the advanced nations as a whole, however, demand expansion is not a solution; indeed, it will only add new problems.

The second and somewhat more controversial proposition of the not-quite consensus is that the growth of international trade is not the main cause of the persistent rise in European unemployment and American inequality. Rather, the main source is a decline in the internal demand for less-skilled labor, probably driven in large part by technological change biased toward highly skilled workers. While Kapstein insists that time should not be wasted debating causes, he nonetheless finds time to pick sides in the dispute here, asserting that "as a general explanation, technology is unsatisfactory. It is never clearly distinguished from other kinds of capital, and there is no reason that its introduction must in principle reduce the wages of the unskilled."

In fact, MIT's Robert Solow won a Nobel Prize in economics in large part for making it very clear why technological progress and capital accumulation are not at all the same—and how to measure the difference. Since his work, in literally thousands of empirical studies of economic change, the distinction between technology and capital has played a crucial role. (My own article in the November/December 1994 *Foreign Affairs*, "The Myth of Asia's Miracle," was motivated by this very distinction.)

But Kapstein is quite right that technology need not in principle reduce the wages of the unskilled. Whether it does so depends on the bias of the technological change—whether it is sufficiently biased toward skilled and against unskilled workers. But the claim of many economists that technological change is a major factor in recent wage trends is not based on a priori reasoning; it is an empirical proposition, based on facts. Nearly all industries (including those not exposed to international competition) have been increasing the average skill level of their work force by hiring relatively more skilled workers, despite the lower wages of unskilled workers. That indicates that recent technological change has been strongly skill-biased.

The conventional view that international trade is only a secondary source of the growth in unemployment and inequality is also an empirical proposition, and one not arrived at lightly. This is an ongoing debate, driven by technical issues rather than ideology. It is risky for nonspecialists to put their faith in an economist merely because they like the sound of what the economist says. For example, Adrian Wood's work, approvingly cited by Kapstein, has been subjected to devastating criticism; Wood's own numbers do not support his strong claims, and he arrives at large estimates of trade's effect only by finessing a basic calculation that indicates the opposite conclusion.[1]

Does the distinction between internal and international causes matter? Yes, it does. Although Kapstein forswears protectionism, it is not at all clear why. After all, if international trade is the main cause of the problem, why not use import restrictions as one line of defense? But if international trade is only 10 or 20 percent of the problem, a protectionist response will bring a whole new set of problems without resolving the ones we already have.

WHAT TO DO

Suppose the middle-of-the-road position on unemployment and inequality is correct: the main source of these problems is a structural, not cyclical, decline in the internal demand for less-skilled labor within advanced countries. One may then conclude that neither a simple policy of overall demand expansion nor one of protectionism against Third World imports is the answer. What, then, can be done?

This is actually not such a hard question. In the United States, which has managed to maintain relatively full employment but has experienced rising inequality, the incomes of low-wage workers need support; but that must be done, so far as possible, without raising the cost to employers of hiring those workers. The obvious answer is something like a much bigger version of the earned income tax credit—an income supplement for workers with low earnings that falls off as a worker's earnings rise, but not so rapidly as to negate pay increases and discourage work. Such a program would be subject to some abuse, but so are all government programs.

Europe has nearly the opposite problem. The poor receive relatively generous support, but not enough people are employed. What Europe needs to do is reduce the cost of employing the less skilled, so that the private sector will offer them more jobs. But it must do so without, so far as possible, reducing their incomes. In this case reducing or removing the tax burden associated with hiring low-wage labor, and possibly providing some employment subsidies, are the obvious answers.

The important point—on which I agree with Kapstein—is that it should be possible to make a large difference to the incomes of low-wage workers (in the United States) or to their prospects of employment (in Europe) without devastating effects on the budget. In the United States, the crucial thing to remember is just how poor the poor are and how rich the country is. If the United States were willing to devote, say, two percent of GDP to income supplements for the working poor, the effect would be dramatic.

So why hasn't the United States tried this policy? Surely it is not because economists have quarreled over whether trade explains 10 or 30 percent of the increase in wage disparities. A better target for Kapstein's ire might be influential figures who insist that the only way to help the poor in America is to cut taxes on the rich. But Kapstein at least

[1]For a detailed dissection of Wood's work, see William Cline, *Trade and Wage Inequality*, Washington: Institute for International Economics, forthcoming. The majority view that technology is the main story while trade is a secondary factor may be wrong, but one certainly should not take sides on this subject unless one is thoroughly familiar with the technical issues involved.

seems to place most of the blame on those with what he regards as a misguided, indeed mystical, concern over budget deficits.

FEAR IS NOT THE ONLY DANGER

Kapstein implies that the economic difficulties of the West are due to its governments' obsession with deficit reduction. Let me repeat that the West's economic problems have been building steadily for more than 20 years, while serious budget-cutting has begun only within the last two or three. The term "Eurosclerosis" dates not from the 1990s but from the late 1970s; European unemployment had already risen to double digits by 1985, when budget difficulties were rarely discussed. The Reagan administration took a remarkably relaxed view of unprecedented peacetime deficits during the 1980s, but that fiscal expansion did not prevent inequality in the United States from soaring.

Nor is concern about deficits the reason Western nations have been unwilling to provide more support for low-wage workers. The sums involved are small enough that if governments and voters were truly persuaded that such policies were necessary, they could quite easily be funded with new taxes or reduced benefits to middle- and upper-income families. Governments and voters are not persuaded, but that has nothing to do with the deficit.

The main reason Kapstein is eager to put aside concern about deficits seems to be that, in spite of all the evidence, he is determined to view the 1990s through the lens of the 1930s. He quotes economist Robert Eisner on the desirability of deficit-induced demand. But with the possible exception of Japan, every advanced country has plenty of room to increase demand simply by cutting interest rates. If they do not do so, it is because their central bankers think an increase in demand is unnecessary or dangerous. They might be wrong, but running budget deficits, which will merely lead those central bankers to impose still higher interest rates, will do nothing to help the situation.

Still, would a more relaxed attitude toward budget deficits do any harm? Here Kapstein's article becomes truly mischievous, by suggesting that concern about deficits is motivated entirely by ideology. Would that it were! Unfortunately, the West is past the point at which the virtues and vices of its budget deficits could be discussed in terms of uncertain macroeconomic effects. The stakes now are much cruder and more elemental: the long-term solvency of Western governments.

Debt as a percentage of national income in almost all Western nations is now comparable to the levels that historically have prevailed only at the end of major wars. But there has been no war, and instead of paying down their debts, as peacetime governments always have in the past, Western treasuries are continuing to increase their debt, for the most part faster than the increases in their tax bases. Moreover, in the current situation there are no major emergencies—no big arms races or wars in prospect, no natural disasters that require extraordinary spending. But stuff happens. If governments cannot control their budgets when it is not happening, what will they do when it does?

The demographic time bomb makes this situation particularly worrying. The budgets of advanced countries are in large part engines that transfer money from workers to retirees, a system that runs smoothly as long as the population is steadily growing, so that the working-age population is large relative to the retired population. But Western populations have not grown steadily. Baby boom was followed by baby bust, and it is therefore certain that the demands on the social insurance systems of advanced countries will greatly exceed their resources beginning only a bit more than a decade from now. Or to put it differently, to the already huge explicit debts of Western nations one should add implicit debt in the form of their unfunded promises to future retirees. In short, concern about the budget deficits of Western nations can no longer be considered a matter of ideology. These days it is a matter of straightforward accounting, and one must deliberately stick one's head in the sand to imagine otherwise.

PUBLICITY COORDINATION

The aspect of Kapstein's prescriptions I found most puzzling is his insistence that a prerequisite for effective action is coordination of economic policies among the major economies. His suggestion seems to be fairly close to the textbook model for macroeconomic coordination. In that much-beloved classroom exercise, each country would like to expand its domestic demand but fears that such an expansion will worsen its trade balance or lead to a depreciation of its currency. In that case a coordinated expansion offers a way out. Increased imports are matched by increased exports, and flight capital has nowhere to go. It is a perfectly reasonable scenario in principle. It may even be a good model for the economic situation during the 1930s. But does this story about the need for coordinated expansion bear any resemblance to the current situation?

Let's get specific. Which major economies are actually constrained from expansion by concerns about the balance of payments or the reaction of international financial markets? Surely not the United States, which may huff and puff about trade conflicts but whose monetary and fiscal policies treat the trade balance and the exchange rate with benign neglect. Surely not Japan, which is worried about an excessive trade surplus, not a deficit, and which is plagued by a yen that is too strong, not too weak. Japan would actually welcome a bit of capital flight. Surely not Germany; with the deutsche mark the key currency of what remains of the European Monetary System, Germany can expect its neighbors to match any reduction it chooses to make in its interest rates. Probably not Britain; since it stopped pegging the value of the pound in 1992, Britain has felt free to follow an independent monetary policy. If it has tightened recently, it is not because it fears the reaction of international markets, but because its domestic economy is again showing signs of inflationary pressures.

What we are left with, I guess, is France, which is indeed pursuing a more restrictive monetary policy than it would if it were not concerned about the value of the franc. But the reason for France's concern is not any inherent need to keep the franc strong—inflation is almost zero—but precisely the commitment of the French government to the Maastricht criteria. France, in other words, is the victim of too much international coordination, not too little. So Kapstein's demand for coordinated economic policy seems to arise more from his general sense that such coordination ought to be a good thing than from any consideration of the real economic situation. Still, does it do any harm?

Whatever your assessment of the economic case, there is one overwhelming empirical observation that can be made about macroeconomic policy coordination: it never happens. Well, hardly ever. Whole forests have been leveled to print reports about the Plaza, the Louvre, the Group of Seven, and so on, but it is hard to find a single case in which a major economic player has altered monetary or fiscal policy at the behest of the other major players. One often hears about the G-7 process; the reason aficionados like to talk so much about the process is that there have been so few results.

To say, as Kapstein does, that "international policy coordination is necessary so that countries can develop expansionary policies within a collective framework," is in effect to say that real action should be postponed for years while countries engage in endless rounds of content-free summitry. Perhaps if there were a compelling case for coordinated policies there might be a way to turn these photo ops into real negotiations (although recent experience in noneconomic affairs is not encouraging), but there is no such compelling case.

None of this should be taken as a counsel of inaction. There is a great deal that can be done to improve the economic situations of the ill-paid and unemployed. However, there is no reason to tie responsible, realistic proposals to raise incomes and create jobs either to irresponsible demands for bigger deficits or to unrealistic expectations about international coordination.

PAUL KRUGMAN *is Professor of Economics at Stanford University.*

Resist the Binge

ROBERT Z. LAWRENCE

Kapstein is correct in saying that the problems of workers in the developed world are serious. I agree, too, that ignoring their plight could have tragic political consequences. But by overstating the effects of the world economy and ignoring the other sources of these problems, Kapstein could well promote the tragedy he seeks to avoid. I also take strong exception to his proposal that governments increase spending. Expansionary fiscal policy would severely set back the progress governments are finally making in bringing their expenditures in line with their revenues. First, expansion driven by a fiscal stimulus is not needed. To the degree that there is insufficient demand in the developed countries—in Europe and Japan, but not the United States—domestic monetary policies are quite adequate for the task. Second, demand-side expansion can do little to solve the structural supply-side problems about which Kapstein is concerned. Economic growth is fundamentally limited by the expansion of productive capacity. Any demand expansion beyond that capacity will translate purely into inflation.

WAGGING THE DOG

Kapstein argues strongly that serious labor market problems such as slow productivity growth, growing inequality, and rising unemployment in the developed countries reflect the increasing influence of the world economy on local conditions. As every student of statistics knows, however, correlation should not be confused with causation. Globalization has increased at a time of poor domestic performance, but is globalization truly culpable or just an innocent bystander?

Globalization is important in Western economies. International trade and investment have expanded rapidly, but consider some facts about the United States. Eighty-eight percent of the goods and services Americans buy, they produce themselves. Eighty-two percent of Americans are employed in sectors like government, construction, nonprofit organizations, services, utilities, and wholesale and retail trade, in which international trade is barely a factor. Moreover, America's international interaction with developing countries remains even smaller. In 1994, U.S. non-oil imports from developing countries amounted to just 3 percent of GNP; exports to developing countries were just 2.5 percent. Employment in the foreign affiliates of U.S. multinationals in developing countries is less than 5 percent of overall U.S. manufacturing employment. I am not saying this interaction has not grown rapidly or even that its effect at the margin may not be greater than these numbers suggest, but to point only to trade with developing countries as the source of workers' problems is to wag a very large dog with a rather small tail.

Most problems in the developed economies would exist even if those economies were not increasingly open to trade and investment. Similarly, most of the remedies require changes in domestic policies unconstrained by international forces. By focusing on the convenient scapegoat of international trade, Kapstein gives short shrift to other important problems, some unique, some shared, that developed countries confront. He overlooks the fact that in the United States, slow domestic productivity growth in service sectors not exposed to trade has led to wage stagnation; that in Europe, sclerotic labor markets and overextended government regulations inhibit structural change, regardless of whether the source is internal or external; and that in Japan, the current recession reflects the aftermath of a splurge sparked by domestic monetary policy, and the recession's persistence stems from failures to deregulate domestic markets and deal with a domestic banking crisis. Kapstein is also too cavalier about the fact that in all countries these problems have been compounded because technological change has shifted demand away from the less-skilled and less-educated workers.

With very few exceptions, economists who have studied the impact of trade with developing countries on labor markets conclude it plays a relatively minor role.[2] In the 1980s, during which Americans experienced widening inequality in their income levels, neither the quantities of imported goods nor the changes in prices the imports caused were large enough to give trade much of a role. Even those in

[2]For a more extensive discussion, see my *Single World, Divided Nations? The Impact of Trade on OECD Labor Markets,* Washington: Brookings Institution, forthcoming.

the United States who believe trade to be significant suggest it explains no more than a fifth of the growth in the relative wages of educated workers. Almost all economists assign a much larger role to the technological changes associated with the introduction of computers and to the changes in management practices that have skewed demand toward more skilled workers while at the same time providing disappointing increases in productivity.

Kapstein dismisses studies by me and others with the claim that trade induces technological change. He argues that "a significant share of new technology, for example, has been induced by foreign competition." In fact, research on the effects of trade on both productivity growth and research-and-development spending confirms the maxim: sometimes a kick in the pants gets you going, and sometimes it just hurts. Some firms, typically in concentrated industries with surplus profits, are spurred to innovate and to spend more on research and development. But other firms, especially those in highly competitive industries, are more likely to respond to international competition by cutting back on investment. It turns out that most trade with developing countries occurs in sectors such as clothing and footwear that are highly competitive. This suggests that when it comes to trade with developing countries, the innovation caused directly by trade is relatively small; indeed, it is more likely to be slowed by trade than sped up. Moreover, to the extent that some trade does lower the wages of unskilled workers throughout the economy, it discourages labor-saving innovation.

Kapstein's account of the role of trade is also imprecise. Does he have in mind all international trade or just trade with developing countries? Since wages in developed countries are quite similar, it must be developing countries he has in mind when he invokes the Stolper-Samuelson theory to argue that trade lowers the welfare of the least-skilled workers in the developed countries. But at another point he talks about the investment-generating effects of trade in industries such as automobiles and steel, in which the developing countries are not major players.

THE GROWTH CEILING

I share with Kapstein the view that government should assist workers in adjusting to change. Training and education are crucial in helping workers adjust, but it is impractical and unrealistic to see them as the only answer. I also concur that the tax system should be used to boost the incomes of the working poor and facilitate job turnover. Europe's strength is that it helps its poor; its problem is that its inflexible labor markets fail to create jobs. America's strength is its flexibility and job creation; its problem is that the income of the least-skilled workers has been depressed. The ideal system would combine American efficiency with European compassion. A deregulated labor market and a generous earned income tax credit would do exactly that. Let wages be freely determined in the market, but let the government safeguard the workers through the tax system.

Where I part company with Kapstein is on his call for coordinated expansionary fiscal policies. Indeed, I think his prescription of tight money and loose fiscal policies has it exactly wrong. Loosen money, perhaps, but keep fiscal policy tight. Currently, there may be some room in Europe and Japan for monetary expansion and, in my heretical view, in countries such as France even room for exchange rates to float. But soon this expansion in demand will strike the ceiling set by the supply capacity of the economy. In a fully employed economy, that capacity is equal to the rise in output per worker plus the growth of the labor force. Once that ceiling is reached, efforts to expand demand can only produce inflation. There is some controversy over whether the United States has already reached the maximum growth rate. I would err on the side of caution, but if you think more stimulus is called for, leave it up to the Federal Reserve. However, calling for bigger budget deficits and more public works programs could not be more wrongheaded. If the problem is slow productivity growth, the country surely needs more investment. But change the mix and not the size of public spending. Let fiscal policy contribute to supply growth by substituting public investment for public consumption, but not through bigger deficits. Increased government borrowing leads to higher interest rates and crowds out private investment. Public works programs delay market adjustments and fail to give workers the skills they need for viable long-run employment. Moreover, such fiscal expansion reinforces the tendency to deny the need for adjustments by piling up debt for future generations.

The simple truth is that, notwithstanding Kapstein's pronouncement, monetary and fiscal policies cannot "be structured in such a way as to ensure . . . that working people can earn a living wage." Successful fiscal and monetary policies may keep inflation low and achieve full employment, but only increased productivity in the private sector can raise the marketplace earnings of working people. If these earnings are inadequate, redistribution may have a role. But bigger government deficits will only pass the burden to future generations.

ROBERT Z. LAWRENCE *is Albert L. Williams Professor of International Trade and Investment at the John F. Kennedy School of Government, Harvard University.*

Mollycoddled

HILARY BARNES

Kapstein's "Workers of the World" was interesting but wrong-headed. First, he implicitly equates workers of the world with workers of only the industrial world. They indeed may have something to worry about with the globalization of the economy, but there are billions of workers in other countries who have reason to be happy about what is happening. Second, Kapstein seems to think that deficit spending and monetary stimulus would generate growth and reduce unemployment. But this is the path the industrial countries went down between about 1946 and 1980. They learned that it does not work, and that it would certainly do nothing to solve the U.S. productivity problem. Third, in Europe at least, the notion that governments have broken the postwar contract with workers—full employment and comprehensive social welfare—is only half right. Full employment is gone, but not social welfare. In fact, social welfare is so comprehensive that it is no longer a solution; it is the problem.

In the part of the world from which this response comes, a large portion of the working-age population obtains very little or no financial benefit from taking a job as opposed to exploiting the social welfare system. Governments no longer have coherent policies for employment, only policies against unemployment, which are not the two sides of the same coin one might think. They fight unemployment by setting up programs to lift people off the dole, education programs, leave-from-work-at-taxpayers'-expense programs, early retirement programs, you name it. Cosmetically, these programs support the politically potent slogan, "We have reduced unemployment." But that is an illusion.

INEQUALITY HAS ITS PLACE

One of the great contemporary worries, reflected in Kapstein's article, is that income differentials are widening. But in Scandinavia, the lifetime income of a youngster who leaves school at 16 to become a cashier in a supermarket will be much the same as the lifetime income of an engineer. The modern Swedish economy was built by its engineers, but today Sweden has fewer engineers per capita than South Korea, and the Swedish economy is going downhill fast. It may be unfashionable to say so, but income differentials have their place.

Reform in Europe requires more flexible labor markets and fewer privileges for trade unions. It also requires changes in the social welfare system, but change is extremely difficult. About two-thirds of the voting population in Scandinavia is on the government payroll, either as a government employee or a client of the welfare state. Tampering with this source of income is politically explosive.

One country that seems to have been able to carry out successful reforms is New Zealand, but European politicians generally dismiss those reforms as irrelevant. I realized why when I asked a very senior Scandinavian social democrat if New Zealand hadn't pointed the way. "Yes, but look what happened to the party, the New Zealand Labour Party, that initiated the reforms. Do you think we are going to risk the same fate?" Ultimately, seen from this corner of the world, Kapstein may be right, but for the wrong reasons. Workers are not disaffected. They are mollycoddled. But if failure to reform labor markets and social welfare systems causes the economies of the advanced European welfare states to collapse, the disaffection of a large part of the electorate, and not just the workers, may well cause political mayhem.

HILARY BARNES, *Nordic Correspondent for* The Economist *and Copenhagen Correspondent for the* Financial Times, *is Editor of* The Scandinavian Economies.

Across the Tracks

THOMAS DONAHUE

Three cheers for Ethan Kapstein for opening a debate on how to address the needs of workers in the so-called global village. He accurately details the good intentions of the framers of post–World War II economic policy and their expressed concern not only that economic reform produce jobs and income growth, but also that mechanisms be created to assist those displaced by trade, changes in technology, or the growth of newly industrialized and developing economies.

In analyzing the early successes and later failures of those mechanisms in the United States, he could also have noted the drying up and practical disappearance of trade adjustment assistance, as successive Republican administrations attempted to eliminate it from the budget; the slashing of worker training and adjustment funds; and the blind dedication of Republican and Democratic administrations alike to "free trade" along lines quite different from those envisioned in the 1947 Havana Charter's call for addressing unfair labor conditions within the international trade regime. These retrenchments have convinced workers in the United States and other developed nations that they are the only people paying the price for economic change in the world and for small improvements in the conditions of workers in developing nations. Meanwhile, workers in the underdeveloped world continue to be exploited by First, Second, and Third World employers alike.

Kapstein has also put in clear focus the absurdity of blaming technology for job losses simply because economists have been unwilling or unable to demonstrate other causes, and the equal absurdity of espousing job training as a magic bullet when job creation is the only real answer. The supply-side idea failed as an economic theory, and it has been no better as an employment program.

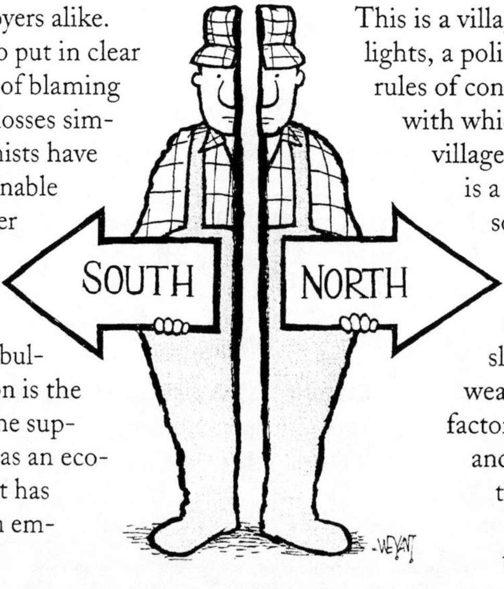

THIS IS NOT 'OUR TOWN'

The truth about trade, free trade, and all recent trade negotiations is that none of them can occur in isolation from other economic acts. Negotiating for free trade and opening up markets makes absolutely no sense without consideration of labor markets, exchange rates, government regulations, capital movements, and so on. Unfortunately, free trade has been pushed as the Vitamin E, the all-purpose cure-all, by economic elites who have been further enriched by it, often at the expense of workers.

The global village is a great phrase. It conjures up the image of an American New England town or midwestern village of the idealized past—friendly people, shared values, opportunity for everyone, children at school and play growing up secure in the embrace of the "village." As a slogan for globalism, it's an ad man's delight. As a reality, however, it must be examined a little more closely, for the global village bears no resemblance to the one in *Our Town*. This is a village without street lights, a police force, or any rules of conduct or standards with which the people in the village can identify. This is a village where, on some of the back streets, children as young as five or six work as bonded slaves in carpet weaving, in clothing factories, and in quarries and mines. Some of the young girls are sold into prostitution. In other manufacturing facilities, workers are badly exploited, with little pay and little or no attention to their health and safety or to environmental damage. On Main Street, along the blocks of fancy retail stores, the products of the back streets sell well to people who would certainly not approve of the abuse of workers, but most of them have never been to the other side of town. The conditions there simply have not intruded on their middle-class consciences. The village council, which has no real power, has created some committees to look at these issues, but they are rarely able to agree on anything other than the concepts of "free trade" and the "free exchange of goods." Their nostrum for the abuses and evils some people hint are the byproducts of free markets is to have still freer markets and more exchanges of goods.

The village council members seem to hear only the analyses offered by the well-to-do merchants and other elites of the village, all of whom seem to be prospering rather nicely, thank you. They occasionally discuss rules of conduct, but their agreements are years in the making and are generally at the level of the lowest common denominator. The truth is, this global village of ours is not a village at all. It remains a world of 190 or so independent and sovereign nations, each trying to get an advantage for itself (and hopefully its citizens), and one in which only the strongest among them, in concert with a few others, can hope to do so. What they have in common is that they are capital-starved and capital-sensitive. They know that capital can move around the world in seconds, and they know they must try to attract it amid very strong competition, with jobs and investments going to those whose wage rates are low and whose environmental and labor standards are either soft or nonexistent. Small wonder, then, that they are frightened by any talk—from within or without—about raising standards, about human rights and worker rights, and about trade sanctions or any other mechanism to enforce any kind of standards or rights. That is the real picture of the global village, and it is not a place you or I should want to live.

TOO MUCH FAITH IN FREE TRADE

In Kapstein's phrase, "growing income inequality, job insecurity, and unemployment are widely seen as the flip side of globalization," and the political debate over what to do about them "will soon turn sour," resulting in xenophobia and pressure for protectionism. A part of the answer does lie in "easing pressures on the 'losers' of the new open economy" with a renewed emphasis on growth, training, education, public job creation, and sharply more progressive income taxes. But the fundamental change that must take place, if there is to be prosperity in the long run, is in the simplistic faith in free trade and free markets. The challenge for the United States and other nations is to devise trade policies and to manage trade in ways that help their citizens within limits that other nations will find tolerable. Trade negotiations must be aimed at establishing rules of fairness, not just openness, and rules for managing trade, currency, and investment flows in ways that begin to redress the enormous imbalance between rich and poor in the world. If that is not done, there can never be real peace and stability.

Basic to redressing that imbalance is an American insistence on trade rules that guarantee the observance in all nations of internationally accepted rights of freedom of association and collective bargaining, health and safety standards, and prohibitions of child labor. These standards have already been developed by the International Labor Organization. The World Trade Organization should make them a requirement for all trade. Successive U.S. administrations have supported this goal—with varying degrees of energy or enthusiasm—but recent efforts have shown that the necessary support among a critical mass of other nations may now be available. If the new U.S. trade representative can secure agreement in the WTO for such standards, the world might for the first time be on its way to a trading system that benefits ordinary people. With that, and with expansionary international economic policies, we might avert the calamities that surely lie ahead on the overly narrow free trade road we have followed for too long.

THOMAS DONAHUE *is former President of the AFL-CIO and former Chairman of the Labor Advisory Committee to the U.S. Trade Representative.*

Unleashing Growth

STEVE FORBES

Kapstein has no need for pessimism. The United States and other advanced industrial countries could easily grow at significantly faster rates than they do now. These countries are on the cusp of a new era that will fundamentally alter the way people live and work, enriching their lives not only materially but spiritually and culturally as well. The transition to this new era doesn't have to be anything like the disruptive, wrenching process industrial nations went through as they changed from agrarian to machine-based economies.

The microchip is extending the reach of the human brain the way machines, beginning nearly two centuries ago, have extended the reach of human muscle. Take one of the early examples of the microchip age—the calculator, which is ubiquitous, cheap, and easy to use. All of us are now in a sense math geniuses in that we can quickly carry out mathematical computations that 50 years ago would have taken math whizzes hours or days to complete. And no one has to be left behind. Just go to a supermarket checkout counter, where the very sophisticated inventory technology can be mastered rapidly by just about anyone.

TAXES EXACT A PRICE

The obstacles to fully realizing the potential of this new economy while minimizing any disruptive elements are removable and reformable. All it takes is insight and political will. The principal barrier to progress is nations' tax codes, most of which are not only unnecessarily complex but have high marginal rates that impose needless burdens on the economy. What too many policymakers and economists cannot seem to grasp is that taxes are not only a means of raising revenue, but also a price. Taxes on income, profits, and capital gains are the price for working and being innovative, productive, and successful. Lower the price on these good things and there will be more of them.

Cumbersome, often foolish regulation is another unnecessary burden. America's formidable progress in digital communications, for example, is slowed because regulators and politicians will not let telephone and cable companies combine to wire homes. Computer chips can now handle billions of bits of information per second, while telephone wires can transmit only a few thousand. Hence graphics are maddeningly slow on the Internet, and moving pictures have a jerky quality. Cable wire and fiber optics can handle the volume of data computers require, yet because of regulations, one cannot easily connect a telephone to a cable wire.

In Europe, regulations and labor restrictions frequently are even more ferociously burdensome than they are in the United States, and tax burdens are far heavier. That is why unemployment remains intractably high, growth is anemic, and technological innovation and new business formation are, by American standards, almost nonexistent. Europe needs a dose of Ludwig Erhard–like tax cuts-cum-simplification-and-deregulation. For its part, America is hurt by a substandard education system and an increasingly arbitrary, lottery-like legal system. And the generous welfare systems of Europe, like that of the United States, are undermining the very qualities that enable people to get ahead. While the frequency of murder and rape in Europe is still far behind that in America, rates for robberies and burglaries in many European countries now match or exceed ours.

AN ANTSY FED

The prescriptions are straightforward, particularly major deregulation and significant tax reductions and tax simplification. A new Bonn Summit, on the other hand, is not necessary. There is no need for grand attempts at coordination among major nations that at best will be clumsy and ineffective. If the United States does it right, most nations will quickly follow its lead.

The choice that many economists cite between more inflation and more prosperity is a false one. We can have both sound money and healthy growth, as the West generally did in the 1950s and most of the 1960s. Easy money is like a drug—you need more and more of the fix to get high, and the reckoning is invariably painful. But there is a vast difference between price changes that reflect supply and demand and price changes that reflect debasement of the currency. Too many central bankers now believe that growth rates in excess of 2 or 3 percent are inflationary and unsustainable, and the Federal Reserve gets antsy anytime growth exceeds 2.5 percent for a couple of quarters. This is preposterous. Historically, the U.S. economy has grown at a 3.5 percent clip, and the fundamentals are there for a few years of growth equal to that of the early and mid-1960s.

Since the early 1980s, with only a few interruptions, the United States has had an investment boom, making it the world's leading manufacturer. Chrysler, which six years ago was on the financial ropes, now makes more money in one year than the entire Japanese auto industry. The United States is the world's high-tech leader in software, fiber optics, Internet technology, microprocessors, and biotechnology. Real worker compensation is also going up, albeit too slowly. Growing income inequality is more of a social phenomenon than an economic one—a divorced woman raising children almost invariably suffers a sharp drop in her financial well-being. Moreover, studies such as a recent one by the Federal Reserve Bank of Dallas demonstrate what any observer should already know: the American economy is extraordinarily dynamic. Most of those in the bottom quintiles in the early 1980s had moved up, while nearly 40 percent of those in the top quintile had suffered a relative decline.

The dynamic of the machine age was bigness—big companies, big cities, big unions, big government. The dynamic of the microchip era is the opposite—antihierarchical, antiauthoritarian, and profoundly individualistic. The role of government is now a negative one of removing tax and regulatory barriers. The real source of anxiety in the developed world is the fear that those who lose their jobs will not be able to find comparable or better ones. A rapidly growing economy, which Western countries are quite capable of achieving, would allay most of those fears. Such an economy would also see a far healthier rise in personal incomes.

STEVE FORBES *is President and CEO of Forbes, Inc.*

Political Economy

ETHAN B. KAPSTEIN

In *The General Theory of Employment, Interest, and Money,* Keynes wrote of the power that classical economic theory still had over his discipline during the 1930s, a period remembered as the Great Depression: "That it could explain much social injustice and apparent cruelty as an inevitable incident in the scheme of progress, and the attempt to change such things as likely on the whole to do more harm than good, commended it to authority. That it afforded a measure of justification to the free activities of the individual capitalist, attracted to it the support of the dominant social force behind authority."

Like their predecessors, today's trade duo of Paul Krugman and Robert Z. Lawrence conservatively call on governments to "do no harm." They would have us believe that a priestly sect of economists has reached something like a consensus regarding the effects of globalization on workers. This simply is not true. As two economists wrote in response to a famous paper by Lawrence and Matthew Slaughter, "The link between international trade and relative wage behavior remains an open issue." In seeking to monopolize the debate, Krugman and Lawrence denigrate "nonspecialists" like me, who allegedly lack an understanding of the "technical issues" surrounding economic matters. I suppose that in their view working people would also have no right to debate economic policy, just as the soldiers in *All Quiet on the Western Front* had no right to discuss the conduct of World War I with officers. In taking this line they remind us of the Edward Tellers who once scoffed at efforts by such amateurs as political scientists, religious leaders, lay citizens, and yes, even economists to influence defense policy, much less arms control, during the 1950s and 1960s. Fortunately, an increasing number of economists are troubled by the yawning gap between their theories and reality. As Stephen Roach of Morgan Stanley recently stated, contemporary economic policies have a "fatal flaw," in that "they are built on the back of hollowing out labor."

WRONG PRIORITIES

My purpose here is not to elaborate on the crisis in modern economic theory. It is instead to remind my critics that societal outcomes ultimately reflect the pulling and hauling of political processes, and this is as true for economic policy as it is for health care or defense. All of us seem to agree that many workers are on the losing end of contemporary economic change. This outcome, I argue, did not arise spontaneously but as the consequence of a change in policy priorities—priorities that now relegate workers to the back seat. I agree with Steve Forbes and Hilary Barnes when they say that Europe's labor markets need reform, but labor must have a voice in that process. Indeed, what is lacking in Europe is a viable political strategy for renegotiating the postwar bargain. Economists would do themselves an analytical favor if they put the "political" back into economy.

Krugman and Lawrence say that the villain in the story is technical change, and again, nowhere do the economists define what they mean by technology. But let's simplify the story—as economists like to do—and define technology as computers. The widespread introduction of computers in industry, they say, has had a bias against unskilled labor, thus lowering wages in the United States and causing unemployment in Europe. They accuse me of being a closet protectionist, but this argument makes them closet Luddites. If technological change is hurting workers, why on earth would we encourage such investment? In the event, that's exactly what we do. Tax policy favors investment in "capital" (including technology) but not labor. Do we have the balance right?

I suppose they would agree with me that while we should encourage technical change, we must at the same time compensate those who lose in the process. This compensation, however, costs money, and here their position as deficit hawks is awkward. Krugman, for example, calls on the United States to devote "say, two percent of GDP to income supplements for the working poor." Two percent of GDP is a big number—it's over $100 billion, substantially more than the $80 billion I suggest in my article as a first step—especially at a time when welfare, education, and training programs are being cut. Does he really believe that the U.S. Congress would appropriate these funds? And if so, does he believe it could be done in the current climate of balancing the budget? Krugman's spending plan gives his contention that my "mischievous" proposals would spur inflation and render Western governments insolvent a hollow ring. I of course agree that money must be spent on these problems and, indeed, that it should be a national priority. I would also prefer to change the composition of government spending rather than increase the deficit. But I would rather help working people now than not, in the face of those who say the budget must first be balanced.

Krugman and Lawrence assert that the limits of noninflationary growth have been reached and that trust should be put in the leadership of the Federal Reserve. But the definition of noninflationary unemployment has changed over time; today it is somewhere between five and six percent, but at an earlier time it was lower. Would they really wish to conclude that nothing can be done for the unemployed or underemployed in this country, especially among youth, women, and minorities where the numbers are still high? Is an expansion of the already existing earned income tax credit the best that 200 years of accumulated economic knowledge can offer to workers? If so, is it any wonder that nonspecialists like me are entering the fray? In this light it is interesting that other nonspecialists like Forbes are questioning the limits-of-growth theme.

ECONOMISTS NEVER LEARN

The economists' disconnect from the world of politics is evident throughout their comments. For example, Krugman criticizes the parallels I draw between the 1990s and the 1930s. What he does not seem to understand is that it is European leaders who are drawing those parallels, not I. The reason Kohl and Chirac are pushing so hard for a monetary union—which Krugman, curiously, seems to oppose—is that they fear an outbreak of the very beggar-thy-neighbor economic policies that characterized and deepened the depression. Being of an older—and wiser—generation, they still believe that international economic policy coordination can be a force for peace and prosperity. The paradox is that in pushing for monetary union on the one hand they are undermining domestic social welfare programs on the other, thus eroding political support for the union they wish to achieve. The great challenge of contemporary European politics revolves around dealing with this paradox, and I would argue that the United States really does have a dog in that fight. After all, it was the breakdown of European politics that caused the two great world wars of this century. Doesn't the United States have a national interest in promoting global economic growth, given this historical record?

Economics is vastly more sophisticated today than it was in Keynes' time. It uses mathematical models that even specialists trained in an earlier era find difficult to understand. But there is little evidence that it has become wiser as a discipline. Lawrence says that economic policy cannot be structured in such a way as to help people earn a living wage. If that is so, what is the point? That is the very question with which Keynes struggled his entire career, and his victory over classical economics came only after a depression and a world war. Is that what it will take for a new Keynes to arise in our midst?

ETHAN B. KAPSTEIN *has recently been appointed the Stassen Professor of International Peace at the University of Minnesota.*

Global Public Policy

Wolfgang H. Reinicke

GOING GLOBAL

GIVEN THE widespread use of the term globalization, it is surprising how little we know about it. In most cases, it is asserted but never defined. Those who do describe it characterize it as a continuous increase of cross-border financial and economic activities leading to greater economic interdependence. Essentially, interdependence and globalization are used interchangeably. This creates a paradox: the same term that is understood as a mere quantitative rise in a trend going back to the 1960s is also used to refer to a fundamental qualitative change in the international system, predicting perhaps the end of the nation-state. If the former is true, there is little need for governments to reassess their role, or that of the institutions and principles that have governed the world economy since the end of World War II, in view of globalization. If the latter holds, it becomes necessary to draw a distinction between economic interdependence and globalization, a distinction that provides a basis for reassessing the role of government and governance in an emerging global economy.

Unlike interdependence, which narrowed the distance between sovereign states and caused closer macroeconomic cooperation, globalization is a microeconomic phenomenon. Globalization represents the integration of a cross-national dimension into the very nature of the organizational structure and strategic behavior of individual companies. The cross-border movement of intangible capital, such as finance, technology, and information, allows companies to enhance their competitiveness.

Wolfgang H. Reinicke is a Senior Scholar in the Foreign Policy Studies Program at the Brookings Institution. This article is based on his forthcoming book, *Global Public Policy: Governing Without Government?*

While in the 1960s and 1970s foreign direct investment closely correlated with world output and trade, it expanded at an average of 16 percent annually between 1985 and 1995, compared with 2 percent and 7 percent, respectively, for output and trade. Most of this additional investment was concentrated in the countries of the Organization for Economic Cooperation and Development and a few developing countries and consisted of mergers and acquisitions in research and development-intensive industries. Controlling for the opening of both China and the former Soviet bloc, which attracted almost no investment before 1985, the share of foreign direct investment going to the developing world actually dropped. The pattern of corporate alliances and collaborative agreements confirms this picture. Such alliances have multiplied during the last decade, and close to 90 percent have occurred in OECD countries.

These changes have had qualitative implications for international trade, which increasingly is structured and restructured by foreign direct investment and international alliances. Today about 70 percent of world trade is intra-industry or intra-firm. Both are closely tied to global corporate strategies, and neither has much to do with the textbook case of comparative advantage. The mid-1980s advent of securitization transformed the financial world, facilitating global corporate strategies, giving foreign debtors and creditors access to domestic financial markets, and contributing to the skyrocketing growth of cross-border capital flows during the last decade. In particular, the market for derivative instruments has led to greater growth and volatility of international capital flows. In 1995 the combined annual value of global trade and foreign direct investment amounted to only six days of turnover on the global foreign exchange markets.

These data show that much of the past decade's international economic activity reflects the internal but cross-border restructuring of corporate activities. In many cases, corporations absorb foreign capital stock, enveloping economic activities that were once conducted on the open market. Alliances such as long-term supplier agreements and licensing and franchising contracts are also not fully exposed to market forces. Globalization is resulting in the emergence of a single integrated economy shaped by corporate networks and their financial relationships. Reliable data for intra-firm trade exist only for the

United States, but in 1994 this off-market trade accounted for approximately 40 percent of total U.S. trade. Governments continue to register these internal transfers not because they are traded but because they cross borders. Although the practice is widespread, equating globalization with the emergence of a global market economy can be misleading.

Interdependence was an important precursor of globalization. It led to the creation of international regimes like the General Agreement on Tariffs and Trade and the International Monetary Fund and it was an important causal factor in encouraging globalization. Like technological innovation, the deregulation and liberalization of cross-border economic activity fostered an environment that not only permitted but compelled companies to adopt global strategies. The public policy response by governments to increased interdependence cannot also be its consequence. Before considering policy responses to globalization, it is necessary to examine the challenges globalization presents to governments and how they differ from those of interdependence.

THREATENING DEMOCRACY

GLOBALIZATION CHALLENGES sovereignty, but so did interdependence. Neither interdependence nor globalization can challenge the legal sovereignty of a state—only other states can. If anything, these forces challenge the operational sovereignty of a government, that is, its ability to exercise sovereignty in the daily affairs of politics. Sovereignty has two dimensions, internal and external. The internal dimension is the relationship between the state and civil society. Following Max Weber, a government is internally sovereign if it enjoys a monopoly of the legitimate power over a range of social activities, including economic ones, within a given territory. That power is embodied in the domestic legal, administrative, and political structures that guide public policies. With respect to the economy, internal sovereignty takes effect when governments collect taxes or regulate private sector activities.

The external dimension of sovereignty refers to relationships among states in the international system. These relationships are defined by the absence of a central authority. As Thomas Hobbes put it, anarchy is the rule of the international system. External economic sovereignty comes into play when, for example, countries collect tariffs and alter their exchange rates. Economic interdependence challenges this dimension of state sovereignty. Governments have responded by following the principles of liberal economic internationalism, endorsing the gradual reduction of their external economic sovereignty by lowering tariffs and capital controls.

Global corporate networks challenge a state's internal sovereignty by altering the relationship between the private and public sectors. By inducing corporations to fuse national markets, globalization creates an economic geography that subsumes multiple political geographies. A government no longer has a monopoly of the legitimate power over the territory within which corporations operate, as the rising incidence of regulatory and tax arbitrage attests. By no means does this imply private sector actors are always deliberately undermining internal sovereignty. Rather, they follow a different organizational logic than states, whose legitimacy derives from their ability to maintain boundaries. Markets, however, do not depend on the presence of boundaries. While globalization integrates markets, it fragments politics.

The threat to a government's ability to exercise internal sovereignty implies a threat to democracy. Although individuals may exercise their right to vote, the power of that vote in shaping public policy decreases along with a state's internal sovereignty. Persistent weakness in internal sovereignty will cast doubt on democratic institutions. It is an important factor in the declining trust in democratic institutions of governance and one to which governments must respond.

PUBLIC POLICY WITH BORDERS

POLICYMAKERS ARE likely to respond to challenges to internal sovereignty in two ways, variants on what is essentially an interventionist strategy. Defensive intervention relies on economic measures such as tariffs, nontariff barriers, and capital controls, forcing companies to reorganize along national lines. If economic nationalism fails to arouse broad popular support, its political counterpart—territorial secession and partition—may do so. Alternatively, policymakers can intervene offensively with subsidies or competitive deregulation. Under these circumstances, states themselves become global competitors, seeking to entice corporations to set up shop within their territory. Among

OECD countries, subsidies grew 27 percent from 1989 to 1993 and competitive deregulation has become common among financial centers and, more recently, among national tax jurisdictions. The use of offensive intervention has increased as policymakers attempt to broaden the reach of internal sovereignty to match the economic reach of corporate networks. Two recent examples are the Helms-Burton Act and California's attempt to impose its unitary tax code on companies like Barclays and Colgate-Palmolive.

None of these responses bodes well for international relations. Protectionism by one country, irrespective of its intentions, leads to retaliation and jeopardizes the world economy. Subsidizing an industry to gain competitive advantage will not advance integration, but rather divert scarce public funds from important public policy goals. Competitive deregulation may not lead to disintegration, but it defeats the original purpose of the policy; a fully deregulated market further reduces a government's internal sovereignty. Extraterritoriality is no friend of deeper integration either. Other states will retaliate against a dictate. Finally, redefining political geography through partition only gives the appearance of greater control of policy. Partitioning a country focuses exclusively on the external dimension of sovereignty. In no way does it insulate governments from the challenges of globalization. If anything, it makes them more vulnerable.

All these responses emphasize territoriality as an ordering principle of international relations, a condition that integration has tried to overcome and that the end of the Cold War appeared to have secured. All are at odds with globalization and will succeed only if the achievements of interdependence are reversed. The popularity of these policies has increased considerably since the early 1990s. In many countries, political opportunists have taken advantage of the public's fear concerning the declining effectiveness of internal sovereignty. Unless policymakers find a better alternative, governments may be forced into these counterproductive measures to halt the loss of internal sovereignty and the further erosion of confidence in democratic institutions.

NEW PARTNERS

ANY ALTERNATIVE strategy must avoid the pitfalls of territoriality. Forming a global government is one response, but it is unrealistic. It would require states to abdicate their sovereignty not only in daily affairs but in a formal sense as well. A more promising strategy differentiates governance and government. Governance, a social function crucial for the operation of any market economy, does not have to be equated with government. Accordingly, global public policy uncouples governance from the nation-state and government.

To implement such a strategy, policymakers would delegate tasks to other actors and institutions that are in a better position to implement global public policies—not only to public sector agencies like the World Bank and the IMF, but also business, labor, and nongovernmental organizations. These groups not only have a stake in the outcome and better information, but have a boundless range of activity. Such public-private partnerships would increase the legitimacy of global public policy and produce a more efficient and effective policy process. Whether grappling with global financial regulation, environmental protection, transnational law enforcement, the control of dual-use technology, or other issues, public-private partnerships could provide the foundation for global public policy.

Critics of such an approach will correctly question the wisdom of placing private and public interests under the direction of the same institution, charging that the public's interest is likely to be neglected. The limited experience with mixing public and private regulation at the national level supports these skeptics. But rather than abandoning global public policy, the current shortcomings of mixed regulation should be addressed. First, greater transparency is necessary. Strict principles of disclosure and guaranteed access for interested parties would raise public confidence. Second, corporations must facilitate public-private partnerships by improving their own internal control and management structures. Independent audits and incentives that discourage excessive risk are examples. The better these controls, the lower the risk of market failure and the need for outside regulation. Those with doubts about public-private partnerships and global public policy should consider the danger of the alternatives.

KEEPING UP WITH THE TIMES

GIVEN THE still limited reach of globalization, international relations remains characterized by the coexistence of interdependence and globalization, cutting across countries and industries. Globalization dominates relationships between advanced industrial countries. The increasing focus on nontariff barriers ranging from financial regulation to health, environmental, and safety standards is a telling example. Interdependence remains the rule for industrializing countries. External sovereignty and territorial interests remain important factors in determining their foreign policy. In North-South relations, the coexistence of interdependence and globalization is reflected in the changing mandate of international organizations such as the World Trade Organization, which no longer focuses exclusively on free trade but has been pressed by the industrialized countries to pursue free trade with an eye to environmental protection and minimum labor standards. The dynamics of interdependence and globalization also coexist in individual economic sectors, such as financial services. At the same time that industrialized countries, through the IMF, the WTO, and the OECD, are encouraging developing nations to deregulate and liberalize their financial markets, they are attempting to establish global public policies that can respond to the consequences of the deregulation and liberalization of their own financial services industries.

The coexistence of interdependence and globalization is not yet reflected in the world's approach to a growing number of transnational policy issues. At a minimum, the institutions of interdependence, such as the IMF, and of globalization, such as the Joint Forum, which brings together regulators from the banking, securities, and insurance industries, should cooperate much more closely. In many cases, policy efforts to promote interdependence and global public policy may best be located under one roof. A united effort would help avoid bureaucratic overlap and turf fights between international institutions and permit a more integrated approach to developing economies' dual challenge of national liberalization and global public policy.

As for the security ramifications of the now largely interdependent and rapidly globalizing world, it will no longer suffice for the architects of international security to view international relations along traditional lines. The coexistence of interdependence and globalization places new demands on international security. Combining external and internal sovereignty in a constructive way will be a significant challenge. Whereas external sovereignty depends on the ability to exclude, internal sovereignty depends on the ability to include.

While globalization integrates markets, it fragments politics.

The shifting demands on international security will also transform the domestic politics of security policy. The challenges emanating from globalization do not usually threaten a country's overall security or territorial integrity. The threats are diffuse and seldom directed at an entire country, often challenging specific groups and in some cases individuals. These threats come from global networks of nonstate actors in domains as diverse as communication, finance, technology, and transport. Anticipating and measuring them will be difficult, as will mustering support for collective national responses to them. Policy coalitions to counter these new threats will transcend national boundaries, calling into question the very concept of national security.

As globalization reaches more countries, international institutions charged with security management will have to expand their ability to handle issues of internal sovereignty. The debate over the future of NATO is a case in point. Opponents of NATO enlargement focus on external sovereignty, emphasizing the policy's territorial consequences. Proponents stress internal sovereignty, recasting the alliance's mission as the promotion of democracy and civil society. Given the political bias in favor of enlargement, whether or not NATO should be enlarged may be the wrong question. The real question is whether NATO members are prepared to choose the right mix of external and internal sovereignty, one that reflects the changing composition of European and global security demands and engages Russia.

The need for inclusiveness extends beyond NATO enlargement. The data on foreign direct investment and corporate alliances demonstrate that large parts of the world economy remain excluded from globalization. With internal sovereignty becoming an issue of international relations, this suggests a strategic vision that places the international financial institutions, such as the IMF and the World Bank, and regional development organizations at the center of future international security. The World Bank has already begun to shift its attention to aspects of internal sovereignty, including good governance, poverty reduction, and conflict prevention, and it should continue in that direction. The IMF has begun to focus on such matters as global financial system regulation, money laundering, tax collection, and corruption. By drawing attention to the economic consequences of excessive military spending, both institutions have questioned a country's requirements for the preservation of external sovereignty when basic elements of internal sovereignty can no longer be financed. Five decades ago these institutions were given the mandate to manage growing interdependence. Their future lies in the management of globalization and global public policy. Without adjustments, the institutions will not be in a position to pursue this new mandate, let alone rationalize their continued existence.

Globalization's success depends on North-South transfers of capital.

For now it should be clear that globalization's success depends on North-South transfers of capital, tangible and intangible alike. In 1990, 44 percent of all long-term financial flows to developing countries came from private sources, the remainder being public financial flows. By 1996, the share of private financial flows had increased to 86 percent. The bulk of North-South transfers will continue to come from the private sector. But if global public policy is to succeed, it requires public funds. Without this assistance, developing countries will not be able to participate too. Renewed calls for development assistance may seem vain, given the difficulty rationalizing foreign aid after the Cold War. But resource transfers to promote global public policy are neither foreign nor aid, but an investment that provides returns to all.

TOWARD A GLOBAL PUBLIC POLICY

INTERNATIONAL RELATIONS is at a crossroads. The interventionist strategies outlined above should not be dismissed as politically ill-fitting. Such strategies are increasingly popular, as seen in the last French election, the Iran-Libya Sanctions Act, and Quebec's attempt at secession. Consequently, external sovereignty will once again come to dominate relations between states, ultimately increasing the risk of territorial conflict.

The alternative scenario, global public policy, does not contest internal sovereignty as an organizing principle, but it does contest its territoriality. It demands political leadership and institutional change, both of which are in short supply. It also requires the willingness of private and nongovernmental actors, especially in the global corporate community, to cooperate closely and share responsibility in implementing public policy while ensuring democratic principles.

The world economy consists of a growing number of global corporate networks. The current state of global governance, however, resembles at best a cross-national policy patchwork, conspicuous for its missing links and unnecessary overlaps. If global public policy is to be an alternative to interventionism, governments must ensure that these patchworks evolve into networks of governance. Their first step should be to commission a global governance audit that would map global obligations and responsibilities along different dimensions, including functional, financial, institutional, and structural. The New York-based Center on International Cooperation has recently initiated an effort along those lines.

The next step would be to fill the most important gaps identified in each policy area. National bureaucracies, not just the top leadership, need to establish permanent channels of communication on cross-border economic activity. The recent failures of financial regulation evidenced in the case of Barings and Daiwa Banks confirm the need for such networking, but it must go far beyond the domain of global financial markets. Policymakers should meet periodically to share experiences and techniques. Greater cooperation between international institutions would prevent unnecessary duplication of activities and an agreed-on division of labor on global governance could contain turf fights that have erupted in recent years. The December 1996 agreement on collaboration between the IMF and the WTO is a welcome start. But as the World Bank's experience in the former Yugoslavia has shown, the exchange of information and coordination of activities must extend to humanitarian and security organizations, such as NATO and the Organization for Security and Cooperation in Europe, which are also confronted with the challenges of eroding internal sovereignty.

The nation-state as a sovereign actor will become a thing of the past.

Finally, while multigovernment networks are a precondition for global public policy, they are by no means the only one. Unless governments and international organizations create and use cross-national structures of public interest, global public policy cannot emerge. In policy areas such as environmental protection, humanitarian assistance, and financial regulation, support for such structures has grown. But too often this support came as a hasty reaction to a crisis and not as part of a well-executed strategy. Cross-national social networks will signal the foundation of a global civil society and be vital to the legitimacy and accountability of global public policy.

Probing further into the future, including the future of the nation-state itself, one must recognize that globalization has ended the nation-state's monopoly over internal sovereignty, which was formerly guaranteed by territory. Outsourcing anarchy to the international system, as Hobbes did, will no longer guarantee internal sovereignty at home. This change deprives external sovereignty of its functional value.

The nation-state as an externally sovereign actor in the international system will become a thing of the past. But this will only happen if internal sovereignty is realized through global public policy. This requires political elites to dissociate themselves to some degree from territory and create more dynamic and responsive institutions of governance. Anarchy is no longer just the outcome of, but also the cause for state interests in the international system. Whether and how long this evolving hybrid is called a nation-state should be of little concern. The administration of sovereignty has changed many times over the centuries; the nation-state is a relatively recent form of governance and it has no claim to perpetuity. While the territorial state may eventually become redundant, the principles and values that govern democracies should not. Steps should be taken now to support the notion of global public policy so that society will be better equipped to respond to the demands of globalization.

Power Shift

Jessica T. Mathews

THE RISE OF GLOBAL CIVIL SOCIETY

THE END of the Cold War has brought no mere adjustment among states but a novel redistribution of power among states, markets, and civil society. National governments are not simply losing autonomy in a globalizing economy. They are sharing powers—including political, social, and security roles at the core of sovereignty—with businesses, with international organizations, and with a multitude of citizens groups, known as nongovernmental organizations (NGOs). The steady concentration of power in the hands of states that began in 1648 with the Peace of Westphalia is over, at least for a while.[1]

The absolutes of the Westphalian system—territorially fixed states where everything of value lies within some state's borders; a single, secular authority governing each territory and representing it outside its borders; and no authority above states—are all dissolving. Increasingly, resources and threats that matter, including money, information, pollution, and popular culture, circulate and shape lives and economies with little regard for political boundaries. International standards of conduct are gradually beginning to override claims of national or regional singularity. Even the most powerful states find the marketplace and international public opinion compelling them more often to follow a particular course.

The state's central task of assuring security is the least affected, but still not exempt. War will not disappear, but with the shrinkage of U.S. and Russian nuclear arsenals, the transformation of the

---

JESSICA T. MATHEWS is a Senior Fellow at the Council on Foreign Relations.

Nuclear Nonproliferation Treaty into a permanent covenant in 1995, agreement on the long-sought Comprehensive Test Ban treaty in 1996, and the likely entry into force of the Chemical Weapons Convention in 1997, the security threat to states from other states is on a downward course. Nontraditional threats, however, are rising—terrorism, organized crime, drug trafficking, ethnic conflict, and the combination of rapid population growth, environmental decline, and poverty that breeds economic stagnation, political instability, and, sometimes, state collapse. The nearly 100 armed conflicts since the end of the Cold War have virtually all been intrastate affairs. Many began with governments acting against their own citizens, through extreme corruption, violence, incompetence, or complete breakdown, as in Somalia.

These trends have fed a growing sense that individuals' security may not in fact reliably derive from their nation's security. A competing notion of "human security" is creeping around the edges of official thinking, suggesting that security be viewed as emerging from the conditions of daily life—food, shelter, employment, health, public safety—rather than flowing downward from a country's foreign relations and military strength.

The most powerful engine of change in the relative decline of states and the rise of nonstate actors is the computer and telecommunications revolution, whose deep political and social consequences have been almost completely ignored. Widely accessible and affordable technology has broken governments' monopoly on the collection and management of large amounts of information and deprived governments of the deference they enjoyed because of it. In every sphere of activity, instantaneous access to information and the ability to put it to use multiplies the number of players who matter and reduces the number who command great authority. The effect on the loudest voice—which has been government's—has been the greatest.

By drastically reducing the importance of proximity, the new technologies change people's perceptions of community. Fax machines,

[1]The author would like to acknowledge the contributions of the authors of ten case studies for the Council on Foreign Relations study group, "Sovereignty, Nonstate Actors, and a New World Politics," on which this article is based.

satellite hookups, and the Internet connect people across borders with exponentially growing ease while separating them from natural and historical associations within nations. In this sense a powerful globalizing force, they can also have the opposite effect, amplifying political and social fragmentation by enabling more and more identities and interests scattered around the globe to coalesce and thrive.

These technologies have the potential to divide society along new lines, separating ordinary people from elites with the wealth and education to command technology's power. Those elites are not only the rich but also citizens groups with transnational interests and identities that frequently have more in common with counterparts in other countries, whether industrialized or developing, than with countrymen.

Above all, the information technologies disrupt hierarchies, spreading power among more people and groups. In drastically lowering the costs of communication, consultation, and coordination, they favor decentralized networks over other modes of organization. In a network, individuals or groups link for joint action without building a physical or formal institutional presence. Networks have no person at the top and no center. Instead, they have multiple nodes where collections of individuals or groups interact for different purposes. Businesses, citizens organizations, ethnic groups, and crime cartels have all readily adopted the network model. Governments, on the other hand, are quintessential hierarchies, wedded to an organizational form incompatible with all that the new technologies make possible.

Today's powerful nonstate actors are not without precedent. The British East India Company ran a subcontinent, and a few influential NGOs go back more than a century. But these are exceptions. Both in numbers and in impact, nonstate actors have never before approached their current strength. And a still larger role likely lies ahead.

DIAL LOCALLY, ACT GLOBALLY

NO ONE knows how many NGOs there are or how fast the tally is growing. Published figures are badly misleading. One widely cited estimate claims there are 35,000 NGOs in the developing countries;

another points to 12,000 irrigation cooperatives in South Asia alone. In fact, it is impossible to measure a swiftly growing universe that includes neighborhood, professional, service, and advocacy groups, both secular and church-based, promoting every conceivable cause and funded by donations, fees, foundations, governments, international organizations, or the sale of products and services. The true number is certainly in the millions, from the tiniest village association to influential but modestly funded international groups like Amnesty International to larger global activist organizations like Greenpeace and giant service providers like CARE, which has an annual budget of nearly $400 million.

NGOs are able to push around even the largest governments.

Except in China, Japan, the Middle East, and a few other places where culture or authoritarian governments severely limit civil society, NGOs' role and influence have exploded in the last half-decade. Their financial resources and—often more important—their expertise, approximate and sometimes exceed those of smaller governments and of international organizations. "We have less money and fewer resources than Amnesty International, and we are the arm of the U.N. for human rights," noted Ibrahima Fall, head of the U.N. Centre for Human Rights, in 1993. "This is clearly ridiculous." Today NGOs deliver more official development assistance than the entire U.N. system (excluding the World Bank and the International Monetary Fund). In many countries they are delivering the services—in urban and rural community development, education, and health care—that faltering governments can no longer manage.

The range of these groups' work is almost as broad as their interests. They breed new ideas; advocate, protest, and mobilize public support; do legal, scientific, technical, and policy analysis; provide services; shape, implement, monitor, and enforce national and international commitments; and change institutions and norms.

Increasingly, NGOs are able to push around even the largest governments. When the United States and Mexico set out to reach a trade agreement, the two governments planned on the usual narrowly defined negotiations behind closed doors. But NGOs had a very different vision. Groups from Canada, the United States, and Mexico wanted to see provisions in the North American Free Trade Agreement on health and safety, transboundary pollution, consumer protection, immigration, labor mobility, child labor, sustainable agriculture, social charters, and debt relief. Coalitions of NGOs formed in each country and across both borders. The opposition they generated in early 1991 endangered congressional approval of the crucial "fast track" negotiating authority for the U.S. government. After months of resistance, the Bush administration capitulated, opening the agreement to environmental and labor concerns. Although progress in other trade venues will be slow, the tightly closed world of trade negotiations has been changed forever.

Technology is fundamental to NGOs' new clout. The nonprofit Association for Progressive Communications provides 50,000 NGOs in 133 countries access to the tens of millions of Internet users for the price of a local call. The dramatically lower costs of international communication have altered NGOs' goals and changed international outcomes. Within hours of the first gunshots of the Chiapas rebellion in southern Mexico in January 1994, for example, the Internet swarmed with messages from human rights activists. The worldwide media attention they and their groups focused on Chiapas, along with the influx of rights activists to the area, sharply limited the Mexican government's response. What in other times would have been a bloody insurgency turned out to be a largely nonviolent conflict. "The shots lasted ten days," José Angel Gurría, Mexico's foreign minister, later remarked, "and ever since, the war has been . . . a war on the Internet."

NGOs' easy reach behind other states' borders forces governments to consider domestic public opinion in countries with which they are dealing, even on matters that governments have traditionally handled strictly between themselves. At the same time, cross-border NGO networks offer citizens groups unprecedented channels of influence. Women's and human rights groups in many developing countries have linked up with more experienced, better funded, and more powerful groups in Europe and the United States. The latter work the global media and lobby their own governments to pressure leaders in developing countries, creating a circle of influence that is accelerating change in many parts of the world.

OUT OF THE HALLWAY, AROUND THE TABLE

IN INTERNATIONAL organizations, as with governments at home, NGOs were once largely relegated to the hallways. Even when they were able to shape governments' agendas, as the Helsinki Watch human rights groups did in the Conference on Security and Cooperation in Europe in the 1980s, their influence was largely determined by how receptive their own government's delegation happened to be. Their only option was to work through governments.

All that changed with the negotiation of the global climate treaty, culminating at the Earth Summit in Rio de Janeiro in 1992. With the broader independent base of public support that environmental groups command, NGOs set the original goal of negotiating an agreement to control greenhouse gases long before governments were ready to do so, proposed most of its structure and content, and lobbied and mobilized public pressure to force through a pact that virtually no one else thought possible when the talks began.

More members of NGOs served on government delegations than ever before, and they penetrated deeply into official decision-making. They were allowed to attend the small working group meetings where the real decisions in international negotiations are made. The tiny nation of Vanuatu turned its delegation over to an NGO with expertise in international law (a group based in London and funded by an American foundation), thereby making itself and the other sea-level island states major players in the fight to control global warming. *ECO*, an NGO-published daily newspaper, was negotiators' best source of information on the progress of the official talks and became the forum where governments tested ideas for breaking deadlocks.

Whether from developing or developed countries, NGOs were tightly organized in a global and half a dozen regional Climate Action Networks, which were able to bridge North-South differences among governments that many had expected would prevent an agreement. United in their passionate pursuit of a treaty, NGOs would fight out contentious issues among themselves, then take an agreed position to their respective delegations. When they could not agree, NGOs served as invaluable back channels, letting both sides know where the other's problems lay or where a compromise might be found.

As a result, delegates completed the framework of a global climate accord in the blink of a diplomat's eye—16 months—over the opposition of the three energy superpowers, the United States, Russia, and Saudi Arabia. The treaty entered into force in record time just two years later. Although only a framework accord whose binding requirements are still to be negotiated, the treaty could force sweeping changes in energy use, with potentially enormous implications for every economy.

The influence of NGOs at the climate talks has not yet been matched in any other arena, and indeed has provoked a backlash among some governments. A handful of authoritarian regimes, most notably China, led the charge, but many others share their unease about the role NGOs are assuming. Nevertheless, NGOs have worked their way into the heart of international negotiations and into the day-to-day operations of international organizations, bringing new priorities, demands for procedures that give a voice to groups outside government, and new standards of accountability.

ONE WORLD BUSINESS

THE MULTINATIONAL corporations of the 1960s were virtually all American, and prided themselves on their insularity. Foreigners might run subsidiaries, but they were never partners. A foreign posting was a setback for a rising executive.

Today, a global marketplace is developing for retail sales as well as manufacturing. Law, advertising, business consulting, and financial and other services are also marketed internationally. Firms of all nationalities attempt to look and act like locals wherever they operate. Foreign language skills and lengthy experience abroad are an asset, and increasingly a requirement, for top management. Sometimes corporate headquarters are not even in a company's home country.

Amid shifting alliances and joint ventures, made possible by computers and advanced communications, nationalities blur. Offshore banking encourages widespread evasion of national taxes. Whereas the fear in the 1970s was that multinationals would become an arm of government, the concern now is that they are disconnecting from their home countries' national interests, moving jobs, evading taxes, and eroding economic sovereignty in the process.

The even more rapid globalization of financial markets has left governments far behind. Where governments once set foreign exchange rates, private currency traders, accountable only to their bottom line, now trade $1.3 trillion a day, 100 times the volume of world trade. The amount exceeds the total foreign exchange reserves of all governments, and is more than even an alliance of strong states can buck.

Despite the enormous attention given to governments' conflicts over trade rules, private capital flows have been growing twice as fast as trade for years. International portfolio transactions by U.S. investors, 9 percent of U.S. GDP in 1980, had grown to 135 percent of GDP by 1993. Growth in Germany, Britain, and elsewhere has been even more rapid. Direct investment has surged as well. All in all, the global financial market will grow to a staggering $83 trillion by 2000, a 1994 McKinsey & Co. study estimated, triple the aggregate GDP of the affluent nations of the Organization for Economic Cooperation and Development.

Nowadays governments have only the appearance of free choice when they set out to make rules.

Again, technology has been a driving force, shifting financial clout from states to the market with its offer of unprecedented speed in transactions—states cannot match market reaction times measured in seconds—and its dissemination of financial information to a broad range of players. States could choose whether they would belong to rule-based economic systems like the gold standard, but, as former Citicorp chairman Walter Wriston has pointed out, they cannot withdraw from the technology-based marketplace, unless they seek autarky and poverty.

More and more frequently today, governments have only the appearance of free choice when they set economic rules. Markets are setting de facto rules enforced by their own power. States can flout them, but the penalties are severe—loss of vital foreign capital, foreign technology, and domestic jobs. Even the most powerful economy must pay heed. The U.S. government could choose to rescue the Mexican peso in 1994, for example, but it had to do so on terms designed to satisfy the bond markets, not the countries doing the rescuing.

The forces shaping the legitimate global economy are also nourishing globally integrated crime—which U.N. officials peg at a staggering $750 billion a year, $400 billion to $500 billion of that in narcotics, according to U.S. Drug Enforcement Agency estimates. Huge increases in the volume of goods and people crossing borders and competitive pressures to speed the flow of trade by easing inspections and reducing paperwork make it easier to hide contraband. Deregulation and privatization of government-owned businesses, modern communications, rapidly shifting commercial alliances, and the emergence of global financial systems have all helped transform local drug operations into global enterprises. The largely unregulated multi-trillion-dollar pool of money in supranational cyberspace, accessible by computer 24 hours a day, eases the drug trade's toughest problem: transforming huge sums of hot cash into investments in legitimate business.

Globalized crime is a security threat that neither police nor the military—the state's traditional responses—can meet. Controlling it will require states to pool their efforts and to establish unprecedented cooperation with the private sector, thereby compromising two cherished sovereign roles. If states fail, if criminal groups can continue to take advantage of porous borders and transnational financial spaces while governments are limited to acting within their own territory, crime will have the winning edge.

BORN-AGAIN INSTITUTIONS

UNTIL RECENTLY, international organizations were institutions of, by, and for nation-states. Now they are building constituencies of their own and, through NGOs, establishing direct connections to the peoples of the world. The shift is infusing them with new life and influence, but it is also creating tensions.

States feel they need more capable international organizations to deal with a lengthening list of transnational challenges, but at the same time fear competitors. Thus they vote for new forms of international intervention while reasserting sovereignty's first principle: no interference in the domestic affairs of states. They hand international organizations sweeping new responsibilities and then rein them in with circumscribed mandates or inadequate funding. With states ambivalent about intervention, a host of new problems demanding attention, and NGOs bursting with energy, ideas, and calls for a larger role, international organizations are lurching toward an unpredictable, but certainly different, future.

International organizations are still coming to terms with unprecedented growth in the volume of international problem-solving. Between 1972 and 1992 the number of environmental treaties rocketed from a few dozen to more than 900. While collaboration in other fields is not growing at quite that rate, treaties, regimes, and intergovernmental institutions dealing with human rights, trade, narcotics, corruption, crime, refugees, antiterrorism measures, arms control, and democracy are multiplying. "Soft law" in the form of guidelines, recommended practices, nonbinding resolutions, and the like is also rapidly expanding. Behind each new agreement are scientists and lawyers who worked on it, diplomats who negotiated it, and NGOs that back it, most of them committed for the long haul. The new constituency also includes a burgeoning, influential class of international civil servants responsible for implementing, monitoring, and enforcing this enormous new body of law.

No longer of, by, and for the nation-state, international institutions lurch toward change.

At the same time, governments, while ambivalent about the international community mixing in states' domestic affairs, have driven some gaping holes in the wall that has separated the two. In the triumphant months after the Berlin Wall came down, international accords, particularly ones agreed on by what is now the Organization for Security and Cooperation in Europe and by the Organization of American States (OAS), drew explicit links between democracy, human rights, and international security, establishing new legal bases for international interventions. In 1991 the U.N. General Assembly declared itself in favor of humanitarian intervention without the request or consent of the state involved. A year later the Security Council took the unprecedented step of authorizing the use of force "on behalf of civilian populations" in Somalia. Suddenly an interest in citizens began to compete with, and occasionally override, the formerly unquestioned primacy of state interests.

Since 1990 the Security Council has declared a formal threat to international peace and security 61 times, after having done so only six times in the preceding 45 years. It is not that security has been abruptly and terribly threatened; rather, the change reflects the broadened scope of what the international community now feels it should poke its nose into. As with Haiti in 1992, many of the so-called Chapter VII resolutions authorizing forceful intervention concerned domestic situations that involved awful human suffering or offended international norms but posed little if any danger to international peace.

Almost as intrusive as a Chapter VII intervention, though always invited, election monitoring has also become a growth industry. The United Nations monitored no election in a member state during the Cold War, only in colonies. But beginning in 1990 it responded to a deluge of requests from governments that felt compelled to prove their legitimacy by the new standards. In Latin America, where countries most jealously guard their sovereignty, the OAS monitored 11 national elections in four years.

And monitoring is no longer the passive observation it was in earlier decades. Carried out by a close-knit mix of international organizations and NGOs, it involves a large foreign presence dispensing advice and recommending standards for voter registration, campaign law, campaign practices, and the training of clerks and judiciaries. Observers even carry out parallel vote counts that can block fraud but at the same time second-guess the integrity of national counts.

International financial institutions, too, have inserted themselves more into states' domestic affairs. During the 1980s the World Bank attached conditions to loans concerning recipient governments' policies on poverty, the environment, and even, occasionally, military spending, a once sacrosanct domain of national prerogative. In 1991 a statement of bank policy holding that "efficient and accountable public sector management" is crucial to economic growth provided the rationale for subjecting to international oversight everything from official corruption to government competence.

Beyond involving them in an array of domestic economic and social decisions, the new policies force the World Bank, the International Monetary Fund, and other international financial institutions to forge alliances with business, NGOs, and civil society if they are to achieve broad changes in target countries. In the process, they have opened themselves to the same demands they are making of their clients: broader public participation and greater openness in decision-making. As a result, yet another set of doors behind which only officials sat has been thrown open to the private sector and to civil society.

LEAPS OF IMAGINATION

AFTER THREE and a half centuries, it requires a mental leap to think of world politics in any terms other than occasionally cooperating but generally competing states, each defined by its territory and representing all the people therein. Nor is it easy to imagine political entities that could compete with the emotional attachment of a shared landscape, national history, language, flag, and currency.

Yet history proves that there are alternatives other than tribal anarchy. Empires, both tightly and loosely ruled, achieved success and won allegiance. In the Middle Ages, emperors, kings, dukes, knights, popes, archbishops, guilds, and cities exercised overlapping secular power over the same territory in a system that looks much more like a modern, three-dimensional network than the clean-lined, hierarchical state order that replaced it. The question now is whether there are new geographic or functional entities that might grow up alongside the state, taking over some of its powers and emotional resonance.

The kernels of several such entities already exist. The European Union is the most obvious example. Neither a union of states nor an international organization, the EU leaves experts groping for inadequate descriptions like "post-sovereign system" or "unprecedented hybrid." It respects members' borders for some purposes, particularly in foreign and defense policy, but ignores them for others. The union's judiciary can override national law, and its Council of Ministers can overrule certain domestic executive decisions. In its thousands of councils, committees, and working groups, national ministers increasingly find themselves working with their counterparts from other countries to oppose colleagues in their own government; agriculture ministers, for example, ally against finance ministers. In this sense the union penetrates and to some extent weakens the internal bonds of its member states. Whether Frenchmen, Danes, and Greeks will ever think of themselves first as Europeans remains to be seen, but the EU has already come much further than most Americans realize.

Meanwhile, units below the national level are taking on formal international roles. Nearly all 50 American states have trade offices abroad, up from four in 1970, and all have official standing in the World Trade

Organization (WTO). German *Länder* and British local governments have offices at EU headquarters in Brussels. France's Rhône-Alpes region, centered in Lyon, maintains what it calls "embassies" abroad on behalf of a regional economy that includes Geneva, Switzerland, and Turin, Italy.

Emerging political identities not linked to territory pose a more direct challenge to the geographically fixed state system. The WTO is struggling to find a method of handling environmental disputes in the global commons, outside all states' boundaries, that the General Agreement on Tariffs and Trade, drafted 50 years ago, simply never envisioned. Proposals have been floated for a Parliamentary Assembly in the United Nations, parallel to the General Assembly, to represent the people rather than the states of the world. Ideas are under discussion that would give ethnic nations political and legal status, so that the Kurds, for example, could be legally represented as a people in addition to being Turkish, Iranian, or Iraqi citizens.

> The shift from national to another allegiance will be a cultural and political earthquake.

Further in the future is a proposed Global Environmental Authority with independent regulatory powers. This is not as far-fetched as it sounds. The burden of participating in several hundred international environmental bodies is heavy for the richest governments and is becoming prohibitive for others. As the number of international agreements mounts, the pressure to streamline the system—in environmental protection as in other areas—will grow.

The realm of most rapid change is hybrid authorities that include state and nonstate bodies such as the International Telecommunications Union, the International Union for the Conservation of Nature, and hundreds more. In many of these, businesses or NGOs take on formerly public roles. The Geneva-based International Standards Organization, essentially a business NGO, sets widely observed standards on everything from products to internal corporate procedures. The International Securities Markets Association, another private regulator, oversees international trade in private securities markets—the world's second-largest capital market after domestic government bond markets. In another crossover, markets become government enforcers when they adopt treaty standards as the basis for market judgments. States and NGOs are collaborating ad hoc in large-scale humanitarian relief operations that involve both military and civilian forces. Other NGOs have taken on standing operational roles for international organizations in refugee work and development assistance. Almost unnoticed, hybrids like these, in which states are often the junior partners, are becoming a new international norm.

FOR BETTER OR WORSE?

A WORLD that is more adaptable and in which power is more diffused could mean more peace, justice, and capacity to manage the burgeoning list of humankind's interconnected problems. At a time of accelerating change, NGOs are quicker than governments to respond to new demands and opportunities. Internationally, in both the poorest and richest countries, NGOs, when adequately funded, can outperform government in the delivery of many public services. Their growth, along with that of the other elements of civil society, can strengthen the fabric of the many still-fragile democracies. And they are better than governments at dealing with problems that grow slowly and affect society through their cumulative effect on individuals—the "soft" threats of environmental degradation, denial of human rights, population growth, poverty, and lack of development that may already be causing more deaths in conflict than are traditional acts of aggression.

As the computer and telecommunications revolution continues, NGOs will become more capable of large-scale activity across national borders. Their loyalties and orientation, like those of international civil servants and citizens of non-national entities like the EU, are better matched than those of governments to problems that demand transnational solutions. International NGOs and cross-border networks of local groups have bridged North-South differences that in earlier years paralyzed cooperation among countries.

On the economic front, expanding private markets can avoid economically destructive but politically seductive policies, such as excessive borrowing or overly burdensome taxation, to which governments succumb. Unhindered by ideology, private capital flows to where it is best treated and thus can do the most good.

International organizations, given a longer rein by governments and connected to the grassroots by deepening ties with NGOs, could, with adequate funding, take on larger roles in global housekeeping (transportation, communications, environment, health), security (controlling weapons of mass destruction, preventive diplomacy, peacekeeping), human rights, and emergency relief. As various international panels have suggested, the funds could come from fees on international activities, such as currency transactions and air travel, independent of state appropriations. Finally, that new force on the global scene, international public opinion, informed by worldwide media coverage and mobilized by NGOs, can be extraordinarily potent in getting things done, and done quickly.

There are at least as many reasons, however, to believe that the continuing diffusion of power away from nation-states will mean more conflict and less problem-solving both within states and among them.

For all their strengths, NGOs are special interests, albeit not motivated by personal profit. The best of them, the ablest and most passionate, often suffer most from tunnel vision, judging every public act by how it affects their particular interest. Generally, they have limited capacity for large-scale endeavors, and as they grow, the need to sustain growing budgets can compromise the independence of mind and approach that is their greatest asset.

A society in which the piling up of special interests replaces a single strong voice for the common good is unlikely to fare well. Single-issue voters, as Americans know all too well, polarize and freeze public debate. In the longer run, a stronger civil society could also be more fragmented, producing a weakened sense of common identity and purpose and less willingness to invest in public goods, whether health and education or roads and ports. More and more groups promoting worthy but narrow causes could ultimately threaten democratic government.

Internationally, excessive pluralism could have similar consequences. Two hundred nation-states is a barely manageable number. Add hundreds of influential nonstate forces—businesses, NGOs, international organizations, ethnic and religious groups—and the international system may represent more voices but be unable to advance any of them.

Moreover, there are roles that only the state—at least among today's polities—can perform. States are the only nonvoluntary political unit, the one that can impose order and is invested with the power to tax. Severely weakened states will encourage conflict, as they have in Africa,

Central America, and elsewhere. Moreover, it may be that only the nation-state can meet crucial social needs that markets do not value. Providing a modicum of job security, avoiding higher unemployment, preserving a livable environment and a stable climate, and protecting consumer health and safety are but a few of the tasks that could be left dangling in a world of expanding markets and retreating states.

More international decision-making will also exacerbate the so-called democratic deficit, as decisions that elected representatives once made shift to unelected international bodies; this is already a sore point for EU members. It also arises when legislatures are forced to make a single take-it-or-leave-it judgment on huge international agreements, like the several-thousand-page Uruguay Round trade accord. With citizens already feeling that their national governments do not hear individual voices, the trend could well provoke deeper and more dangerous alienation, which in turn could trigger new ethnic and even religious separatism. The end result could be a proliferation of states too weak for either individual economic success or effective international cooperation.

Finally, fearsome dislocations are bound to accompany the weakening of the central institution of modern society. The prophets of an internetted world in which national identities gradually fade, proclaim its revolutionary nature and yet believe the changes will be wholly benign. They won't be. The shift from national to some other political allegiance, if it comes, will be an emotional, cultural, and political earthquake.

DISSOLVING AND EVOLVING

MIGHT THE decline in state power prove transitory? Present disenchantment with national governments could dissipate as quickly as it arose. Continuing globalization may well spark a vigorous reassertion of economic or cultural nationalism. By helping solve problems governments cannot handle, business, NGOs, and international organizations may actually be strengthening the nation-state system.

These are all possibilities, but the clash between the fixed geography of states and the nonterritorial nature of today's problems and solutions, which is only likely to escalate, strongly suggests that the relative power of states will continue to decline. Nation-states may simply no longer be the natural problem-solving unit. Local government addresses citizens' growing desire for a role in decision-making, while transnational, regional, and even global entities better fit the dimensions of trends in economics, resources, and security.

The evolution of information and communications technology, which has only just begun, will probably heavily favor nonstate entities, including those not yet envisaged, over states. The new technologies encourage noninstitutional, shifting networks over the fixed bureaucratic hierarchies that are the hallmark of the single-voiced sovereign state. They dissolve issues' and institutions' ties to a fixed place. And by greatly empowering individuals, they weaken the relative attachment to community, of which the preeminent one in modern society is the nation-state.

If current trends continue, the international system 50 years hence will be profoundly different. During the transition, the Westphalian system and an evolving one will exist side by side. States will set the rules by which all other actors operate, but outside forces will increasingly make decisions for them. In using business, NGOs, and international organizations to address problems they cannot or do not want to take on, states will, more often than not, inadvertently weaken themselves further. Thus governments' unwillingness to adequately fund international organizations helped NGOs move from a peripheral to a central role in shaping multilateral agreements, since the NGOs provided expertise the international organizations lacked. At least for a time, the transition is likely to weaken rather than bolster the world's capacity to solve its problems. If states, with the overwhelming share of power, wealth, and capacity, can do less, less will get done.

Whether the rise of nonstate actors ultimately turns out to be good news or bad will depend on whether humanity can launch itself on a course of rapid social innovation, as it did after World War II. Needed adaptations include a business sector that can shoulder a broader policy role, NGOs that are less parochial and better able to operate on a large scale, international institutions that can efficiently serve the dual masters of states and citizenry, and, above all, new institutions and political entities that match the transnational scope of today's challenges while meeting citizens' demands for accountable democratic governance.

The Real New World Order

Anne-Marie Slaughter

THE STATE STRIKES BACK

MANY THOUGHT that the new world order proclaimed by George Bush was the promise of 1945 fulfilled, a world in which international institutions, led by the United Nations, guaranteed international peace and security with the active support of the world's major powers. That world order is a chimera. Even as a liberal internationalist ideal, it is infeasible at best and dangerous at worst. It requires a centralized rule-making authority, a hierarchy of institutions, and universal membership. Equally to the point, efforts to create such an order have failed. The United Nations cannot function effectively independent of the major powers that compose it, nor will those nations cede their power and sovereignty to an international institution. Efforts to expand supranational authority, whether by the U.N. secretary-general's office, the European Commission, or the World Trade Organization (WTO), have consistently produced a backlash among member states.

The leading alternative to liberal internationalism is "the new medievalism," a back-to-the-future model of the 21st century. Where liberal internationalists see a need for international rules and institutions to solve states' problems, the new medievalists proclaim the end of the nation-state. Less hyperbolically, in her article, "Power Shift," in the January/February 1997 *Foreign Affairs*, Jessica T. Mathews describes a shift away from the state—up, down, and sideways—to supra-state, sub-state, and, above all, nonstate actors. These new players have multiple allegiances and global reach.

ANNE-MARIE SLAUGHTER is the J. Sinclair Armstrong Professor of International, Foreign, and Comparative Law at Harvard Law School.

Mathews attributes this power shift to a change in the structure of organizations: from hierarchies to networks, from centralized compulsion to voluntary association. The engine of this transformation is the information technology revolution, a radically expanded communications capacity that empowers individuals and groups while diminishing traditional authority. The result is not world government, but global governance. If government denotes the formal exercise of power by established institutions, governance denotes cooperative problem-solving by a changing and often uncertain cast. The result is a world order in which global governance networks link Microsoft, the Roman Catholic Church, and Amnesty International to the European Union, the United Nations, and Catalonia.

The new medievalists miss two central points. First, private power is still no substitute for state power. Consumer boycotts of transnational corporations destroying rain forests or exploiting child labor may have an impact on the margin, but most environmentalists or labor activists would prefer national legislation mandating control of foreign subsidiaries. Second, the power shift is not a zero-sum game. A gain in power by nonstate actors does not necessarily translate into a loss of power for the state. On the contrary, many of these nongovernmental organizations (NGOS) network with their foreign counterparts to apply additional pressure on the traditional levers of domestic politics.

A new world order is emerging, with less fanfare but more substance than either the liberal internationalist or new medievalist visions. The state is not disappearing, it is disaggregating into its separate, functionally distinct parts. These parts—courts, regulatory agencies, executives, and even legislatures—are networking with their counterparts abroad, creating a dense web of relations that constitutes a new, transgovernmental order. Today's international problems—terrorism, organized crime, environmental degradation, money laundering, bank failure, and securities fraud—created and sustain these relations. Government institutions have formed networks of their own, ranging from the Basle Committee of Central Bankers to informal ties between law enforcement agencies to legal networks that make foreign judicial decisions more and more familiar. While political scientists Robert Keohane and Joseph Nye first observed its emergence in the 1970s, today transgovernmentalism is rapidly becoming the most widespread and effective mode of international governance.

Compared to the lofty ideals of liberal internationalism and the exuberant possibilities of the new medievalism, transgovernmentalism seems mundane. Meetings between securities regulators, antitrust or environmental officials, judges, or legislators lack the drama of high politics. But for the internationalists of the 1990s—bankers, lawyers, businesspeople, public-interest activists, and criminals—transnational government networks are a reality. Wall Street looks to the Basle Committee rather than the World Bank. Human rights lawyers are more likely to develop transnational litigation strategies for domestic courts than to petition the U.N. Committee on Human Rights.

> The state is not disappearing, it is disaggregating.

Moreover, transgovernmentalism has many virtues. It is a key element of a bipartisan foreign policy, simultaneously assuaging conservative fears of a loss of sovereignty to international institutions and liberal fears of a loss of regulatory power in a globalized economy. While presidential candidate Pat Buchanan and Senator Jesse Helms (R-N.C.) demonize the U.N. and the WTO as supranational bureaucracies that seek to dictate to national governments, Senators Ted Kennedy (D-Mass.) and Paul Wellstone (D-Mich.) inveigh against international capital mobility as the catalyst of a global "race to the bottom" in regulatory standards. Networks of bureaucrats responding to international crises and planning to prevent future problems are more flexible than international institutions and expand the regulatory reach of all participating nations. This combination of flexibility and effectiveness offers something for both sides of the aisle.

Transgovernmentalism also offers promising new mechanisms for the Clinton administration's "enlargement" policy, aiming to expand the community of liberal democracies. Contrary to Samuel Huntington's gloomy predictions in *The Clash of Civilizations and the New World Order* (1996), existing government networks span civilizations, drawing in courts from Argentina to Zimbabwe and financial regulators from Japan to Saudi Arabia. The dominant institutions in these networks remain concentrated in North America and Western Europe, but their impact can be felt in every corner of the globe. Moreover, disaggregating the state makes it possible to assess the quality of specific judicial, administrative, and legislative institutions, whether or not the governments are liberal democracies. Regular interaction with foreign colleagues offers new channels for spreading democratic accountability, governmental integrity, and the rule of law.

An offspring of an increasingly borderless world, transgovernmentalism is a world order ideal in its own right, one that is more effective and potentially more accountable than either of the current alternatives. Liberal internationalism poses the prospect of a supranational bureaucracy answerable to no one. The new medievalist vision appeals equally to states' rights enthusiasts and supranationalists, but could easily reflect the worst of both worlds. Transgovernmentalism, by contrast, leaves the control of government institutions in the hands of national citizens, who must hold their governments as accountable for their transnational activities as for their domestic duties.

JUDICIAL FOREIGN POLICY

JUDGES ARE building a global community of law. They share values and interests based on their belief in the law as distinct but not divorced from politics and their view of themselves as professionals who must be insulated from direct political influence. At its best, this global community reminds each participant that his or her professional performance is being monitored and supported by a larger audience.

National and international judges are networking, becoming increasingly aware of one another and of their stake in a common enterprise. The most informal level of transnational judicial contact is knowledge of foreign and international judicial decisions and a corresponding willingness to cite them. The Israeli Supreme Court and the German and Canadian constitutional courts have long researched U.S. Supreme Court precedents in reaching their own conclusions on questions like freedom of speech, privacy rights, and due process. Fledgling constitutional courts in Central and Eastern Europe and in Russia are eagerly following suit. In 1995, the South African Supreme Court, finding the death penalty unconstitutional under the national constitution, referred to decisions from national and supranational courts around the world, including ones in Hungary, India, Tanzania, Canada, and Germany and the European Court of Human Rights. The U.S. Supreme Court has typically been more of a giver than a receiver in this exchange, but Justice Sandra Day O'Connor recently chided American lawyers and judges for their insularity in ignoring foreign law and predicted that she and her fellow justices would find themselves "looking more frequently to the decisions of other constitutional courts."

National and international judges are networking, creating new global relationships.

Why should a court in Israel or South Africa cite a decision by the U. S. Supreme Court in reaching its own conclusion? Decisions rendered by outside courts can have no authoritative value. They carry weight only because of their intrinsic logical power or because the court invoking them seeks to gain legitimacy by linking itself to a larger community of courts considering similar issues. National courts have become increasingly aware that they and their foreign counterparts are often engaged in a common effort to delimit the boundaries of individual rights in the face of an apparently overriding public interest. Thus, the British House of Lords recently rebuked the U.S. Supreme Court for its decision to uphold the kidnapping of a Mexican doctor by U.S. officials determined to bring him to trial in the United States.

Judges also cooperate in resolving transnational or international disputes. In cases involving citizens of two different states, courts have long been willing to acknowledge each other's potential interest and to defer to one another when such deference is not too costly. U.S. courts now recognize that they may become involved in a sustained dialogue with a foreign court. For instance, Judge Guido Calabresi of the Second Circuit recently allowed a French litigant to invoke U.S. discovery provisions without exhausting discovery options in France, reasoning that it was up to the French courts to identify and protest any infringements of French sovereignty. U.S. courts would then respond to such protests.

Judicial communication is not always harmonious, as in a recent squabble between a U.S. judge and a Hong Kong judge over an insider trading case. The U.S. judge refused to decline jurisdiction in favor of the Hong Kong court on grounds that "in Hong Kong they practically give you a medal for doing this sort of thing [insider trading]." In

CORBIS - BETTMANN

Let's keep talking: judicial networking is born

response, the Hong Kong judge stiffly defended the adequacy of Hong Kong law and asserted his willingness to apply it. He also chided his American counterpart, pointing out that any conflict "should be approached in the spirit of judicial comity rather than judicial competitiveness." Such conflict is to be expected among diplomats, but what is striking here is the two courts' view of themselves as quasi-autonomous foreign policy actors doing battle against international securities fraud.

The most advanced form of judicial cooperation is a partnership between national courts and a supranational tribunal. In the European Union (EU), the European Court of Justice works with national courts when questions of European law overlap national law. National courts refer cases up to the European Court, which issues an opinion and sends the case back to national courts; the supranational recommendation guides the national court's decision. This cooperation marshals the power of domestic courts behind the judgment of a supranational tribunal. While the Treaty of Rome provides for this reference procedure, it is the courts that have transformed it into a judicial partnership.

Finally, judges are talking face to face. The judges of the supreme courts of Western Europe began meeting every three years in 1978. Since then they have become more aware of one another's decisions, particularly with regard to each other's willingness to accept the decisions handed down by the European Court of Justice. Meetings between U.S. Supreme Court justices and their counterparts on the European Court have been sponsored by private groups, as have meetings of U.S. judges with judges from the supreme courts of Central and Eastern Europe and Russia.

The most formal initiative aimed at bringing judges together is the recently inaugurated Organization of the Supreme Courts of the Americas. Twenty-five supreme court justices or their designees met in Washington in October 1995 and drafted the OCSA charter, dedicating the organization to "promot[ing] and strengthen[ing] judicial independence and the rule of law among the members, as well as the proper constitutional treatment of the judiciary as a fundamental branch of the state." The charter calls for triennial meetings and envisages a permanent secretariat. It required ratification by 15 supreme courts, achieved in spring 1996. An initiative by judges, for judges, it is not a stretch to say that OCSA is the product of judicial foreign policy.

Champions of a global rule of law have most frequently envisioned one rule for all, a unified legal system topped by a world court. The global community of law emerging from judicial networks will more likely encompass many rules of law, each established in a specific state or region. No high court would hand down definitive global rules. National courts would interact with one another and with supranational tribunals in ways that would accommodate differences but acknowledge and reinforce common values.

THE REGULATORY WEB

THE DENSEST area of transgovernmental activity is among national regulators. Bureaucrats charged with the administration of antitrust policy, securities regulation, environmental policy, criminal law enforcement, banking and insurance supervision—in short, all the agents of the modern regulatory state—regularly collaborate with their foreign counterparts.

National regulators track their quarry through cooperation. While frequently ad hoc, such cooperation is increasingly cemented by bilateral and multilateral agreements. The most formal of these are mutual legal assistance treaties, whereby two states lay out a protocol governing cooperation between their law enforcement agencies and courts. However, the preferred instrument of cooperation is the memorandum of understanding, in which two or more regulatory agencies set forth and initial terms for an ongoing relationship. Such memorandums are not treaties; they do not engage the executive or the legislature in negotiations, deliberation, or signature. Rather, they are good-faith agreements, affirming ties between regulatory agencies based on their like-minded commitment to getting results.

National regulators track their quarry through cooperation.

"Positive comity," a concept developed by the U.S. Department of Justice, epitomizes the changing nature of transgovernmental relations. Comity of nations, an archaic and notoriously vague term beloved by diplomats and international lawyers, has traditionally signified the deference one nation grants another in recognition of their mutual sovereignty. For instance, a state will recognize another state's laws or judicial judgments based on comity. Positive comity requires more active cooperation. As worked out by the Antitrust Division of the U.S. Department of Justice and the EU's European Commission, the regulatory authorities of both states alert one another to violations within their jurisdiction, with the understanding that the responsible authority will take action. Positive comity is a principle of enduring cooperation between government agencies.

In 1988 the central bankers of the world's major financial powers adopted capital adequacy requirements for all banks under their supervision—a significant reform of the international banking system. It was not the World Bank, the International Monetary Fund, or even the Group of Seven that took this step. Rather, the forum was the Basle Committee on Banking Supervision, an organization composed of 12 central bank governors. The Basle Committee was created by a simple agreement among the governors themselves. Its members meet four times a year and follow their own rules. Decisions are made by consensus and are not formally binding; however, members do implement these decisions within their own systems. The Basle Committee's authority is often cited as an argument for taking domestic action.

National securities commissioners and insurance regulators have followed the Basle Committee's example. Incorporated by a private bill of the Quebec National Assembly, the International Organization of Securities Commissioners has no formal charter or founding treaty. Its primary purpose is to solve problems affecting international securities markets by creating a consensus for enactment of national legislation. Its members have also entered into information-sharing agreements on their own initiative. The International Association of Insurance Supervisors follows a similar model, as does the newly created Tripartite Group, an international coalition of banking, insurance, and securities regulators the Basle Committee created to improve the supervision of financial conglomerates.

Pat Buchanan would have had a field day with the Tripartite Group, denouncing it as a prime example of bureaucrats taking power out of the hands of American voters. In fact, unlike the international bogeymen of demagogic fantasy, transnational regulatory organizations do not aspire to exercise power in the international system independent of their members. Indeed, their main purpose is to help regulators apprehend those who would harm the interests of American voters. Transgovernmental networks often promulgate their own rules, but the purpose of those rules is to enhance the enforcement of national law.

Traditional international law requires states to implement the international obligations they incur through their own law. Thus, if states agree to a 12-mile territorial sea, they must change their domestic legislation concerning the interdiction of vessels in territorial waters accordingly. But this legislation is unlikely to overlap with domestic law, as national legislatures do not usually seek to regulate global commons issues and interstate relations.

Transgovernmental regulation, by contrast, produces rules concerning issues that each nation already regulates within its borders: crime, securities fraud, pollution, tax evasion. The advances in technology and transportation that have fueled globalization have made it more difficult to enforce national law. Regulators benefit from coordinating their enforcement efforts with those of their foreign counterparts and from ensuring that other nations adopt similar approaches.

The result is the nationalization of international law. Regulatory agreements between states are pledges of good faith that are self-enforcing, in the sense that each nation will be better able to enforce its national law by implementing the agreement if other nations do likewise. Laws are binding or coercive only at the national level. Uniformity of result and diversity of means go hand in hand, and the makers and enforcers of rules are national leaders who are accountable to the people.

BIPARTISAN GLOBALIZATION

SECRETARY OF STATE Madeleine Albright seeks to revive the bipartisan foreign policy consensus of the late 1940s. Deputy Secretary of State Strobe Talbott argues that promoting democracy worldwide satisfies the American need for idealpolitik as well as realpolitik. President Clinton, in his second inaugural address, called for a "new government for a new century," abroad as well as at home. But bipartisanship is threatened by divergent responses to globalization, democratization is a tricky business, and Vice President Al Gore's efforts to "reinvent government" have focused on domestic rather than international institutions. Transgovernmentalism can address all these problems.

Globalization implies the erosion of national boundaries. Consequently, regulators' power to implement national regulations within those boundaries declines both because people can easily flee their jurisdiction and because the flows of capital, pollution, pathogens, and weapons are too great and sudden for any one regulator to control. The liberal internationalist response to these assaults on state regulatory power is to build a larger international apparatus. Globalization thus leads to internationalization, or the transfer of regulatory authority from the national level to an international institution. The best example is not the WTO itself, but rather the stream of proposals to expand the WTO's jurisdiction to global competition policy, intellectual property regulation, and other trade-related issues. Liberals are likely to support expanding the power of international institutions to guard against the global dismantling of the regulatory state.

Here's the rub. Conservatives are more likely to favor the expansion of globalized markets without the internationalization that goes with it, since internationalization, from their perspective, equals a loss of sovereignty. According to Buchanan, the U.S. foreign policy establishment "want[s] to move America into a New World Order where the World Court decides quarrels between nations; the WTO writes the rules for trade and settles all disputes; the IMF and World Bank order wealth transfers from continent to continent and country to country; the Law of the Sea Treaty tells us what we may and may not do on the high seas and ocean floor, and the United Nations decides where U.S. military forces may and may not intervene." The rhetoric is deliberately inflammatory, but echoes resound across the Republican spectrum.

Transgovernmental initiatives are a compromise that could command bipartisan support. Regulatory loopholes caused by global forces require a coordinated response beyond the reach of any one country. But this coordination need not come from building more international institutions. It can be achieved through transgovernmental cooperation, involving the same officials who make and implement policy at the national level. The transgovernmental alternative is fast, flexible, and effective.

A leading example of transgovernmentalism in action that demonstrates its bipartisan appeal is a State Department initiative christened the New Transatlantic Agenda. Launched in 1991 under the Bush administration and reinvigorated by Secretary of State Warren Christopher in 1995, the initiative structures the relationship between the United States and the EU, fostering cooperation in areas ranging from opening markets to fighting terrorism, drug trafficking, and infectious disease. It is an umbrella for ongoing projects between U.S. officials and their European counterparts. It reaches ordinary citizens, embracing efforts like the Transatlantic Business Dialogue and engaging individuals through people-to-people exchanges and expanded communication through the Internet.

DEMOCRATIZATION, STEP BY STEP

TRANSGOVERNMENTAL NETWORKS are concentrated among liberal democracies but are not limited to them. Some nondemocratic states have institutions capable of cooperating with their foreign counterparts, such as committed and effective regulatory agencies or relatively independent judiciaries. Transgovernmental ties can strengthen institutions in ways that will help them resist political domination, corruption, and incompetence and build democratic institutions in their countries, step by step. The Organization of Supreme Courts of the Americas, for instance, actively seeks to strengthen norms of judicial independence among its members, many of whom must fend off powerful political forces.

Individuals and groups in nondemocratic countries may also "borrow" government institutions of democratic states to achieve a measure of justice they cannot obtain in their own countries. The court or regulatory agency of one state may be able to perform judicial or regulatory functions for the people of another. Victims of human rights violations, for example, in countries such as Argentina, Ethiopia, Haiti, and the Philippines have sued for redress in the courts of the United States. U.S. courts accepted these cases, often over the objections of the executive branch, using a broad interpretation of a moribund statute dating back to 1789. Under this interpretation, aliens may sue in U.S. courts to seek damages from foreign government officials accused of torture, even if the torture allegedly took place in the foreign country. More generally, a nongovernmental organization seeking to prevent human rights violations can often circumvent their own government's corrupt legislature and politicized court by publicizing the plight of victims abroad and mobilizing a foreign court, legislature, or executive to take action.

Responding to calls for a coherent U.S. foreign policy and seeking to strengthen the community of democratic nations, President Clinton substituted the concept of "enlargement" for the Cold War principle of "containment." Expanding transgovernmental outreach to include institutions from nondemocratic states would help expand the circle of democracies one institution at a time.

A NEW WORLD ORDER IDEAL

TRANSGOVERNMENTALISM OFFERS its own world order ideal, less dramatic but more compelling than either liberal internationalism or the new medievalism. It harnesses the state's power to find and implement solutions to global problems. International institutions have a lackluster record on such problem-solving; indeed, NGOs exist largely to compensate for their inadequacies. Doing away with the state, however, is hardly the answer. The new medievalist mantra of global governance is "governance without government." But governance without government is governance without power, and government without power rarely works. Many pressing international and domestic problems result from states' insufficient power to establish order, build infrastructure, and provide minimum social services. Private actors may take up some slack, but there is no substitute for the state.

Transgovernmental networks allow governments to benefit from the flexibility and decentralization of nonstate actors. Jessica T. Mathews argues that "businesses, citizens' organizations, ethnic groups, and crime cartels have all readily adopted the network model," while governments "are quintessential hierarchies, wedded to an organizational form incompatible with all that the new technologies make possible." Not so. Disaggregating the state into its functional components makes it possible to create networks of institutions engaged in a common enterprise even as they represent distinct national interests. Moreover, they can work with their subnational and supranational counterparts, creating a genuinely new world order in which networked institutions perform the functions of a world government—legislation, administration, and adjudication—without the form.

These globe-spanning networks will strengthen the state as the primary player in the international system. The state's defining attribute has traditionally been sovereignty, conceived as absolute power in domestic affairs and autonomy in relations with other states. But as Abram and Antonia Chayes observe in *The New Sovereignty* (1995), sovereignty is actually "status—the vindication of the state's existence in the international system." More importantly, they demonstrate that in contemporary international relations, sovereignty has been redefined to mean "membership . . . in the regimes that make up the substance of international life." Disaggregating the state permits the disaggregation of sovereignty as well, ensuring that specific state institutions derive strength and status from participation in a transgovernmental order.

Transgovernmental networks will increasingly provide an important anchor for international organizations and nonstate actors alike. U.N. officials have already learned a lesson about the limits of supranational authority; mandated cuts in the international bureaucracy will further tip the balance of power toward national regulators. The next generation of international institutions is also likely to look more like the Basle Committee, or, more formally, the Organization of Economic Cooperation and Development, dedicated to providing a forum for transnational problem-solving and the harmonization of national law. The disaggregation of the state creates opportunities for domestic institutions, particularly courts, to make common cause with their supranational counterparts against their fellow branches of government. Nonstate actors will lobby and litigate wherever they think they will have the most effect. Many already realize that corporate self-regulation and states' promises to comply with vague international agreements are no substitute for national law.

Globe-spanning networks will strengthen the state in the international system.

The spread of transgovernmental networks will depend more on political and professional convergence than on civilizational boundaries. Trust and awareness of a common enterprise are more vulnerable to differing political ideologies and corruption than to cultural differences. Government networks transcend the traditional divide between high and low politics. National militaries, for instance, network as extensively as central bankers with their counterparts in friendly states. Judicial and regulatory networks can help achieve gradual political convergence, but are unlikely to be of much help in the face of a serious economic or military threat. If the coming conflict with China is indeed coming, transgovernmentalism will not stop it.

The strength of transgovernmental networks and of transgovernmentalism as a world order ideal will ultimately depend on their accountability to the world's peoples. To many, the prospect of transnational government by judges and bureaucrats looks more like technocracy than democracy. Critics contend that government institutions engaged in policy coordination with their foreign counterparts will be barely visible, much less accountable, to voters still largely tied to national territory.

Citizens of liberal democracies will not accept any form of international regulation they cannot control. But checking unelected officials is a familiar problem in domestic politics. As national legislators become increasingly aware of transgovernmental networks, they will expand their oversight capacities and develop networks of their own. Transnational NGO networks will develop a similar monitoring capacity. It will be harder to monitor themselves.

Transgovernmentalism offers answers to the most important challenges facing advanced industrial countries: loss of regulatory power with economic globalization, perceptions of a "democratic deficit" as international institutions step in to fill the regulatory gap, and the difficulties of engaging nondemocratic states. Moreover, it provides a powerful alternative to a liberal internationalism that has reached its limits and to a new medievalism that, like the old Marxism, sees the state slowly fading away. The new medievalists are right to emphasize the dawn of a new era, in which information technology will transform the globe. But government networks are government for the information age. They offer the world a blueprint for the international architecture of the 21st century.

The Global Economy and the Nation-State

Peter F. Drucker

A TRUE SURVIVOR

SINCE TALK of the globalization of the world's economy began some 35 years ago, the demise of the nation-state has been widely predicted. Actually, the best and the brightest have been predicting the nation-state's demise for 200 years, beginning with Immanuel Kant in his 1795 essay "Perpetual Peace," through Karl Marx in "Withering Away of the State," to Bertrand Russell's speeches in the 1950s and 1960s. The latest such prediction by eminent and serious people appears in a book called *The Sovereign Individual* by Lord William Rees-Mogg, former editor of the London Times and now vice chairman of the BBC, and James Dale Davidson, chairman of Britain's National Tax Payers' Union. Rees-Mogg and Davidson assert that for all but the lowest earners the Internet will make avoiding taxes so easy and riskless that sovereignty will inevitably shift to the individual, leaving the nation-state to die of fiscal starvation.

Despite all its shortcomings, the nation-state has shown amazing resilience. While Czechoslovakia and Yugoslavia have been casualties of a changing order, Turkey, a nation that never before existed as such, has become a functioning nation-state. India, rarely united except under a foreign conqueror, is holding together as a nation-state. And every country that emerged from the nineteenth-century colonial empires has established itself as a nation-state, as have all the countries emerging from the breakup of the Eurasian empire forged by

PETER F. DRUCKER is Clarke Professor of Social Science at Claremont Graduate University.

the czars and tied together even more tightly by the czar's communist successors. So far, at least, there is no other institution capable of political integration and effective membership in the world's political community. In all probability, therefore, the nation-state will survive the globalization of the economy and the information revolution that accompanies it. But it will be a greatly changed nation-state, especially in domestic fiscal and monetary policies, foreign economic policies, control of international business, and, perhaps, in its conduct of war.

THE NATION-STATE AFLOAT

CONTROL OF money, credit, and fiscal policy was one of three pillars on which Jean Bodin, the brilliant French lawyer who coined the term "sovereignty," set the nation-state in his 1576 *Six Books of the Republic*. It has never been a sturdy pillar. By the late nineteenth century, the dominant currency was no longer state-minted coins or state-printed bank notes, but credit created by fast-growing privately controlled commercial banks. The nation-state countered with the central bank. By 1912, when the United States established the Federal Reserve System, every nation-state had its own central bank to control the commercial banks and their credit. But throughout the nineteenth century, one nation-state after another put itself (or was put) under the control of the nonnational gold standard, which imposed strict limits on a country's monetary and fiscal policies. And the gold exchange standard, established in the Bretton Woods agreements after World War II, while a good deal more flexible than the pre-World War I gold standard, still did not give individual countries full monetary and fiscal sovereignty. Only in 1973, when President Nixon floated the U.S. dollar, did the nation-state—or so it was claimed—attain full autonomy in monetary and fiscal affairs. Surely governments and their economists had learned enough to use such sovereignty responsibly.

Not many economists—at least in the English-speaking world—want to go back to fixed exchange rates or anything resembling the old system. But even fewer would claim that nation-states have shown skill or responsibility in using their new fiscal and

monetary freedom. Floating currencies, it was promised, would make for stable currencies, with the market controlling exchange rates through constant small adjustments. Instead, there has been no period in peacetime, save the early years of the Great Depression, in which currencies have fluctuated as widely and abruptly as since 1973. Freed from external constraints, governments have gone on spending binges.

The Bundesbank in Germany is practically free from political control and is dedicated to fiscal rectitude. It knew that the spending spree the politicians proposed during the country's reunification was economic folly, and it said so loud and clear. Still the politicians went ahead, gaining short-term popularity while risking long-term economic costs. The Bundesbank predicted everything that has come to pass, including unemployment rates in both East and West Germany not seen since the dying days of the Weimar Republic. It is the same with politicians everywhere; it makes little difference which party is in power or how much it promises to cut or control.

VIRTUAL MONEY

WHILE THE hope that governments will practice self-discipline is fantasy, the global economy imposes new and more severe restraints on government. It is forcing government back into fiscal responsibility. Floating exchange rates have created extreme currency instability, which in turn has created an enormous mass of "world money." This money has no existence outside the global economy and its main money markets. It is not being created by economic activity like investment, production, consumption, or trade. It is created primarily by currency trading. It fits none of the traditional definitions of money, whether standard of measurement, storage of value, or medium of exchange. It is totally anonymous. It is virtual rather than real money.

Virtual money has won in every instance, proving that it is the arbiter of economic policies.

But its power is real. The volume of world money is so gigantic that its movements in and out of a currency have far greater impact than the flows of financing, trade, or investment. In one day, as much of this virtual money may be traded as the entire world needs to finance trade and investment for a year. This virtual money has total mobility because it serves no economic function. Billions of it can be switched from one currency to another by a trader pushing a few buttons on a keyboard. And because it serves no economic function and finances nothing, this money also does not follow economic logic or rationality. It is volatile and easily panicked by a rumor or unexpected event.

One example is the run on the dollar in the spring of 1995, which forced President Clinton to abandon his earlier spending plans and embrace a balanced budget. The run was triggered by the failure of the Republican majority in the Senate to pass a constitutional amendment calling for a balanced budget. Even if the amendment had passed, it would have been meaningless. It was riddled with loopholes and required ratification by 38 states to become law, which at best would have taken many years. But the world's currency traders panicked and started a run on the U.S. dollar. Already undervalued 10 percent against the Japanese yen, the run pushed the dollar down another 25 percent—from 106 yen to the dollar to less than 80—in two weeks. More important, the run caused the near-collapse of the U.S. bond market, on which the United States depends to finance its deficits. The central banks of the United States, England, Germany, Japan, Switzerland, and France instantly swung into concerted action to support the dollar. They failed, losing billions in the attempt. It took the dollar the better part of a year to climb back to its original (still undervalued) exchange rate.

A similar panic-driven run on the French franc in 1981 forced President Mitterrand to abandon promises that had helped get him elected three months earlier. There have been panic runs on the Swedish krona, the British pound, the Italian lira, and the Mexican peso. Virtual money won every time, proving that the global economy is the ultimate arbiter of monetary and fiscal policies.

Currency runs, however, are not the appropriate cure for fiscal irresponsibility. In the case of Mexico, they were worse than the disease. The 1995 run on the peso wiped out six years of hard-won economic gains that had turned the country from a basket case into an emerging economy. But so far there is no other control on fiscal irresponsibility. The only thing that can work is fiscal and monetary policies that free a country from depending on borrowing short-term, volatile world money to cover its deficits. This is likely to require a balanced budget—or something very close to balanced—over any three- or five-year period. And this then puts severe limitations on the nation-state's fiscal and monetary autonomy, which the 1973 floating of exchange rates was supposed to set free for all time.

The process of restoring such nonnational and supranational restraints is well under way. The Eurobank's currency for the entire European Economic Community, planned to be in place before the century's end, would transfer control of money and credit from the individual member states to an independent transnational agency. Another approach, apparently favored by the U.S. Federal Reserve Board, would give a consortium of central banks similar authority, thus maintaining the trappings of national fiscal sovereignty while taking away much of its reality. Both approaches, however, would only institutionalize what has already become an economic reality: basic economic decisions are made in and by the global economy rather than the nation-state.

The unrestrained financial and monetary sovereignty given to the nation-state by floating exchange rates 25 years ago has not been good for government. It has largely deprived government of its ability to say no. It has transferred decision-making power from government to special interest groups. It is largely to blame for the precipitate decline in confidence in and respect for government that has been a conspicuous and disturbing trend in almost every country. Paradoxically, losing its fiscal and monetary sovereignty may make the nation-state stronger rather than weaker.

BREAKING THE RULES

FAR SUBTLER but perhaps even more important is the impact of the global economy's rise on the basic assumptions and theories on which most governments, especially in the West, base their international economic policies. There are any number of signs that something is going on in the world economy that breaks the rules that have been at work for decades.

Why did the dollar fall against the yen by more than 50 percent when President Reagan and the Japanese government agreed to give up the fixed 250:1 yen-to-dollar rate in 1983? While the dollar was indeed overvalued, its purchasing power parity with the yen was around 230. No one expected it to drop below 200 yen. Instead, the dollar went into free fall and did not come to rest until it had lost almost 60 percent of its value against the yen, that is, until it hit 110 yen two years later (only to fall again 10 years later to 80 yen). Why? To this day, here has been no explanation. Even more mysterious, the dollar showed such a sharp fall only against the yen. In fact, it increased its value against some other key currencies. Again, no one anticipated this and no one can explain it.

Reagan and his economic advisers wanted a cheaper dollar so as to eliminate a growing trade deficit with Japan. According to all theory and 200 hundred years of experience, a lower dollar should mean more American exports to Japan and fewer American imports from Japan. Japanese exporters, especially the automobile and consumer electronics manufacturers, went into hysterics and announced that the end of the world had come. American exports did indeed go up sharply, but even more to some countries against whose currencies the dollar gained in value. But Japanese exports to the United States, despite the dollar depreciation, rose even faster than U.S. exports to Japan, so that the U.S. trade deficit with Japan actually went up rather than down. Every time in the last 15 years that the dollar has slid against the yen, the American administration of the day has predicted that Japan's trade surplus with the United States would shrink. Every time the Japanese have screamed that they were ruined. And every time Japan's export surplus has increased almost immediately.

There is no explanation for some of the conundrums of a global economy.

One popular explanation is that Japanese manufacturers are geniuses. But although the major exporters are very sharp, genius cannot overcome a 50 percent drop in revenues in virtually no time. The true explanation is that Japan benefited as much from the lower dollar as it was penalized by it. Japan is the world's largest importer of foodstuffs and raw materials, all of which are priced in dollars. It spends roughly as much on importing these commodities as it earns dollars by exporting finished manufactured goods. An individual Japanese manufacturing company like Toyota may lose because the dollars it gets for its cars exported to the United States earn only half as many yen as before, but for the entire Japanese economy the drop in the dollar's value against the yen was simply a wash.

But this raises another, even more mysterious riddle. What explains why the Japanese did not have to pay more for the commodities they imported? According to all theory and earlier experience, commodity prices in dollars should have gone up as much as the dollar went down. The Japanese should have had to pay as much as they did before the dollar was devalued. If that had happened, as it always had before, there would indeed be no Japanese surplus in trade with the United States. But commodity prices in dollars today are lower than in 1983—and there is no explanation for this either.

There is only one piece of the puzzle that makes sense, but it is even less compatible with traditional international trade theory. The U.S. Department of Commerce estimates that 40 percent or more of goods exported from any developed country go to overseas subsidiaries and affiliates of domestic companies. Officially and legally, they are exports. Economically, they are intracompany transfers. They are machines, supplies, and half-finished goods that have been engineered into the production of the plant or the affiliate abroad and must be continued, whatever the exchange rate. To change this relationship would take years and cost more than foreign exchange savings could possibly recover. Forty percent of what is reported as trade in goods is thus "trade" only as a legal fiction. And that proportion is steadily growing.

International trade theory takes for granted that investment follows trade. Most people think "international trade in goods" when they hear the words "international trade." But increasingly today, trade follows investment. International movements of capital rather than international movements of goods have become the engine of the world economy. And while trade in goods has indeed grown faster since World War II than in any period in history, trade in services has been growing even faster, whether it be financial services, management consulting, accounting, insurance, or retailing. Service exports 20 years ago were so small that they were rarely recorded in trade statistics. Today they are a quarter of U.S. exports and the only producers of sizable American export surpluses. They follow few, if any, of the rules of traditional international trade. Only tourism, for instance, is highly sensitive to foreign exchange rates and their fluctuations.

I have intentionally stuck to American economic conundrums, but similar ones can be found in the economy of every developed country and most developing countries. The centers of the world economy have shifted away from the developed countries. Only 15 years ago it was generally believed that the growth of developing countries depended on the prosperity of the developed ones. In the last two decades, the developed countries have not done particularly well; but world trade and production have boomed as never before, with the bulk of the growth occurring in emerging countries. The explanation, in large part, is that knowledge has replaced the economist's "land, labor, and capital" as the chief economic resource. Knowledge, mainly in the form of the training methods and philosophies developed in the United States during World War II, exploded the axiom that low wages mean low productivity. Training now enables a country's labor force to attain world-class productivity while still paying an emerging country's wages for at least eight or ten years.

These new realities require different economic theories and different international economic policies. Even if a lower exchange rate improves a country's exports, it also weakens a country's ability to invest abroad. And if trade follows investment, lower foreign exchange rates for a country's currency diminish exports within a few years. This is what happened to the United States: the cheaper dollar increased American manufactured exports in the short term. But it also impaired the ability of American industry to invest abroad and thus to create export markets for the long term. As a result, the Japanese are now far ahead of the Americans in market share and market leadership in the emerging countries of East and Southeast Asia.

The need for new theories and policies explains the sudden interest in what is being promoted by James Fallows, editor in chief of *U.S. News and World Report*, and others as the "national development policies" of the nineteenth-century German economist Friedrich R. List. Actually, the policies List preached in 1830s Germany—protection of infant industries so as to develop domestic business—were not List's and were not German. They are strictly American, growing out of Alexander Hamilton's 1791 "Report on Manufactures," which Henry Clay, 25 years later, expanded into what he called the "American System." List, in the United States as a political refugee from Germany, learned them while serving as Clay's secretary.

What makes these old ideas attractive is that Hamilton, Clay, and List did not focus on trade. They were neither free traders nor protectionists. They focused on investment. Asian economies, beginning with Japan after World War II, have been following policies similar to those Hamilton and Clay advocated for the infant United States. The international economic policies likely to emerge over the next generation will be neither free-trade nor protectionist, but focused on investment rather than trade.

SELLING TO THE WORLD

IN THE global economy, businesses are increasingly forced to shift from being multinational to being transnational. The traditional multinational is a national company with foreign subsidiaries. These subsidiaries are clones of the parent company. A German subsidiary of an American manufacturing company, say, is a self-contained operation that manufactures almost everything it sells within Germany, buying its supplies there and employing almost exclusively Germans.

Most companies doing international business today are still organized as traditional multinationals. But the transformation into transnational companies has begun, and it is moving fast. The products or services may be the same, but the structure is fundamentally different. In a transnational company there is only one economic unit, the world. Selling, servicing, public relations, and legal affairs are local. But parts, machines, planning, research, finance, marketing, pricing, and management are conducted in contemplation of the world market. One of America's leading engineering companies, for instance, makes one critical part for all of its 43 plants worldwide in one location outside of Antwerp, Belgium—and nothing else. It has organized product development for the entire world in three places and quality control in four. For this company, national boundaries have largely become irrelevant.

The transnational company is not totally beyond the control of national governments. It must adapt to them. But these adaptations are exceptions to policies and practices decided on for worldwide markets and technologies. Successful transnational companies see themselves as separate, nonnational entities. This self-perception is evidenced by something unthinkable a few decades ago: a transnational top management. The world's best-known management consulting firm, McKinsey & Co., for instance, though headquartered in New York, is headed by an Indian. And for many years the number two man at Citibank, the only big commercial bank that has gone transnational, was Chinese.

The U.S. government is trying to counteract this trend by extending American legal concepts and legislation beyond its shores. It is doing so with respect to antitrust laws, an almost uniquely American concept. It is also trying to rein in transnational companies through American laws covering torts, product liability, and corruption. And America goes to battle against transnational companies through economic sanctions against Cuba and Iraq.

Although the United States is still the world's largest economic power—and likely to remain so for many years—the attempt to mold the world economy to American moral, legal, and economic concepts is futile. In a global economy in which major players can emerge almost overnight, there can be no dominant economic power.

Nonetheless, there is certainly need for moral, legal, and economic rules that are accepted and enforced throughout the global economy. A central challenge, therefore, is the development of international law and supranational organizations that can make and enforce rules for the global economy.

WAR AFTER GLOBAL ECONOMICS

THOUGH INCOMPATIBLE, the global economy and total war are both children of this century. The strategic goal in traditional warfare, in Clausewitz's famous phrase, was "to destroy the enemy's fighting forces." War was to be waged against the enemy's soldiers. It was not supposed to be waged against enemy civilians and their property. There were always exceptions, of course. Sherman's march through Georgia at the end of the U.S. Civil War was aimed at civilians and their property rather than the threadbare Confederate army. But that it was an exception—and meant to be one—is one reason it is still so vividly remembered. A few years later, in the Franco-Prussian War of 1870-71, Bismarck took great care to keep France's financial system intact.

But during this century's first war, the Boer War, the rule was changed. The goal of warfare was redefined as destroying the enemy's potential for waging war, which meant destroying the enemy's economy. Also, for the first time in modern Western history, war was systematically waged against the enemy's civilian population. To break the fighting spirit of the Boer soldiers, the British herded Boer women and children into history's first concentration camps.

Before this century, the West generally observed another rule: enemy civilians residing in one's country were to be left unmolested so long as they did not engage in political activity. But in World War I, Britain and France interned all enemy aliens, although the United States, Germany, and Austria refrained. Until 1900, businesses and property owned by foreign nationals or by companies domiciled in an enemy country were left undisturbed. Since World War I—with the British again taking the lead—such property was confiscated and put under government custodianship in wartime.

The rules of total war are so firmly established by now that most people take them to be akin to laws of nature. With missiles, satellites, and nuclear weapons, there can be no return to the nineteenth-century belief that the military's first task is to keep war away from the country's civilians. In modern war, there are no civilians.

But while destroying the enemy's economy helps win the war, it impairs the victor's chance of winning the peace. This was one of the most significant lessons of this century's two postwar periods, the 20 years after 1918 and the 50 years after 1945. The unprecedented American policies after World War II, including the Marshall Plan, brought about the speedy recovery of the former enemy economies, and with them 50 years of unprecedented economic expansion and prosperity for the victors as well. These policies came into existence because George Marshall, Harry Truman, Dean Acheson, and Douglas MacArthur remembered the catastrophic consequences of World War I's punitive peace. If "war is the continuation of policy by other means," to quote another maxim from Clausewitz, then total war will have to be adjusted to the realities of the global economy.

> Total-war doctrines would harm a country's war effort these days.

Since businesses are moving from multinational to transnational, total-war doctrines may actually be detrimental to a country's war effort these days. For example, Italy's largest armaments producer during World War I was an automobile company named Fiat. Austria-Hungary's largest armaments producer in its fight against Italy during World War I was the wholly owned Austrian subsidiary of Fiat. It had been founded a year or two after the parent company started in Italy, but by 1914 it was substantially larger and more advanced than its parent, owing to the greater size of Austria-Hungary's market. To make this Italian-owned subsidiary the center of Austria's war production required literally nothing but a new bank account.

Today such a wholly owned subsidiary would assemble and sell whole cars, but might only manufacture brakes. That subsidiary's brakes would be used by all the company's plants worldwide, and it would receive all the other parts and supplies it needed from other subsidiaries throughout the world. This transnational integration could cut the costs of the finished automobile by as much as 50 percent. But it also makes an individual subsidiary practically unable to produce anything if cut off from the rest of the company. In many developed countries, businesses integrated transnationally now account for one-third to one-half of their industry's output.

I do not pretend to know the answers to the growing contradiction between peacetime and wartime economies. But there is a precedent. The most innovative political achievement of the nineteenth century was the International Red Cross. First proposed in 1862 by a Swiss citizen, Jean Henri Dunant, it became the world's first transnational agency within 10 years and it is still the world's most successful one. What it did in setting universal rules for treating the wounded and prisoners of war may need to be done now with respect to the treatment of civilians and their property. That too, in all likelihood, will require a transnational agency and, as in the case of the Red Cross, substantial curtailment of national sovereignty.

Since the early Industrial Revolution, it has been argued that economic interdependence would prove stronger than nationalist passions. Kant was the first to say so. The "moderates" of 1860 believed it until the first shots were fired at Fort Sumter. The Liberals of Austria-Hungary believed to the very end that their economy was far too integrated to be split into separate countries. So, quite clearly, did Mikhail Gorbachev. But whenever in the last 200 years political passions and nation-state politics have collided with economic rationality, political passions and the nation-state have won.

Power and Interdependence in the Information Age

Robert O. Keohane and Joseph S. Nye, Jr.

THE RESILIENCE OF STATES

THROUGHOUT THE twentieth century, modernists have been proclaiming that technology would transform world politics. In 1910 Norman Angell declared that economic interdependence rendered wars irrational and looked forward to the day when they would become obsolete. Modernists in the 1970s saw telecommunications and jet travel as creating a global village, and believed that the territorial state, which has dominated world politics since the feudal age, was being eclipsed by nonterritorial actors such as multinational corporations, transnational social movements, and international organizations. Likewise, prophets such as Peter Drucker, Alvin and Heidi Toffler, and Esther Dyson argue that today's information revolution is ending hierarchical bureaucracies and leading to a new electronic feudalism with overlapping communities and jurisdictions laying claim to multiple layers of citizens' identities and loyalties.

The modernists of past generations were partly right. Angell's understanding of the impact of war on interdependence was insightful: World War I wrought unprecedented destruction, not only on the battlefield but also on the social and political systems that had thrived during the relatively peaceful years since 1815. As the modernists of the 1970s predicted, multinational corporations, nongovernmental

ROBERT O. KEOHANE is James B. Duke Professor of Political Science and Co-Director of the Program on Democracy, Institutions, and Political Economy at Duke University. JOSEPH S. NYE, JR., is Dean of the Kennedy School of Government at Harvard University.

organizations (NGOs), and global financial markets have become immensely more significant. But the state has been more resilient than modernists anticipated. States continue to command the loyalties of the vast majority of the world's people, and their control over material resources in most wealthy countries has stayed at a third to half of GDP.

The modernists of 1910 and the 1970s were right about the direction of change but simplistic about its consequences. Like pundits on the information revolution, they moved too directly from technology to political consequences without sufficiently considering the continuity of beliefs, the persistence of institutions, or the strategic options available to statesmen. They failed to analyze how holders of power could wield that power to shape or distort patterns of interdependence that cut across national boundaries.

Twenty years ago, in our book *Power and Interdependence* (1977), we analyzed the politics of such transnational issues as trade, monetary relations, and oceans policy, writing that "modernists point correctly to the fundamental changes now taking place, but they often assume without sufficient analysis that advances in technology and increases in social and economic transactions will lead to a new world in which states, and their control of force, will no longer be important. Traditionalists are adept at showing flaws in the modernist vision by pointing out how military interdependence continues, but find it very difficult accurately to interpret today's multidimensional economic, social, and ecological interdependence." This is still true for the information age in which cyberspace is itself a "place," everywhere and nowhere.

Prophets of a new cyberworld, like modernists before them, often overlook how much the new world overlaps and rests on the traditional world in which power depends on geographically based institutions. In 1998, 100 million people use the Internet. Even if this number reaches a billion in 2005, as some experts predict, a large portion of the world's people will not participate. Moreover, globalization is far from universal. Three-quarters of the world's population does not own a telephone, much less a modem and computer. Rules will be necessary to govern cyberspace, not only protecting lawful users from criminals but ensuring intellectual property rights. Rules require authority, whether in the form of public government or private or community governance. Classic issues of politics—who governs and on what terms—are as relevant to cyberspace as to the real world.

THE EARLY DAYS OF THE REVOLUTION

INTERDEPENDENCE AMONG societies is not new. What is new is the virtual erasing of costs of communicating over distance as a result of the information revolution. The actual transmission costs have become negligible; hence the amount of information that can be transmitted is effectively infinite. Computing power has doubled every 18 months for the last 30 years. It now costs less than one percent of what it did in the early 1970s. Similarly, growth of the Internet and the World Wide Web has been exponential. Internet traffic doubles every 100 days. Communications bandwidths are expanding rapidly, and communications costs continue to fall. As late as 1980, phone calls over copper wire could carry one page of information per second; today a thin strand of optical fiber can transmit 90,000 volumes in a second. As with steam at the end of the eighteenth century and electricity at the end of the nineteenth, productivity growth has lagged as society learns to utilize the new technologies. Although many industries and firms have undergone rapid structural changes since the 1980s, the economic transformation is far from complete. We are still in the early stages of the information revolution.

That revolution has dramatically changed one feature of what we described in *Power and Interdependence* as "complex interdependence"—a world in which security and force matter less and countries are connected by multiple social and political relationships. Now anyone with a computer can be a desktop publisher, and anyone with a modem can communicate with distant parts of the globe at a trivial cost. Earlier transnational flows were heavily controlled by large bureaucracies like multinational corporations or the Catholic Church. Such organizations remain important, but the dramatic cheapening of information transmission has opened the field to loosely structured network organizations and even individuals. These NGOs and networks are particularly effective in penetrating states without regard to borders and using domestic constituencies to force political leaders to focus on their preferred agendas. The information revolution has vastly increased the number of channels of contact between societies, one of our three dimensions of complex interdependence.

However, the information revolution has not made dramatic changes in the two other conditions of complex interdependence. Military force still plays a significant role in relations between states, and in a crunch, security still outranks other issues in foreign policy. One reason that the information revolution has not transformed world politics to a new politics of complete complex interdepence is that information does not flow in a vacuum but in political space that is already occupied. Another is that outside the democractic zone of peace, the world of states is not a world of complex interdependence. In many areas, realist assumptions about the dominance of military force and security issues remain valid. For the last four centuries states have established the political structure within which information flows across borders. Indeed, the information revolution itself can be understood only within the context of the globalization of the world economy, which itself was deliberately fostered by U.S. policy and international institutions for half a century after the end of World War II. In the late 1940s the United States sought to create an open international economy to forestall another depression and contain communism. The resulting international institutions, formed on the basis of multilateral principles, put a premium on markets and information and deemphasized military rivalry. It has become increasingly costly for states to turn away from these patterns of interdependence.

We are still in the early stages of the information revolution.

The quantity of information available in cyberspace means little by itself. The quality of information and distinctions between types of information are probably more important. Information does not just exist; it is created. When one considers the incentives to create information, three different types of information that are sources of power become apparent.

Free information is information that actors are willing to create and distribute without financial compensation. The sender benefits from the receiver believing the information and hence has incentives to produce it. Motives may vary. Scientific information is a public good, but persuasive messages, such as political ones, are more self-serving. Marketing, broadcasting, and propaganda are all examples of free information. The explosion in the quantity of free information is perhaps the most dramatic effect of the information revolution.

Commercial information is information that people are willing to create and send at a price. Senders neither gain nor lose by others believing the information, apart from the compensation they receive. For such information to be available on the Internet, issues of property rights must be resolved so that producers of information can be compensated by users. Creating commercial information before one's competitors can—assuming that intellectual property rights can be enforced—generates enormous profits, especially for pioneers, as the history of Microsoft demonstrates. The rapid growth of electronic commerce and the increase in global competition will be other important effects of the information revolution.

Politics will affect the information revolutio as much as vice versa.

Strategic information, as old as espionage, confers great advantage on actors only if their competitors do not possess it. One enormous advantage the United States had in World War II was that, unbeknown to Tokyo, the United States had broken the Japanese codes. The quantity of such information is often not particularly important. For example, the strategic information available to the United States about the nuclear weapons programs of North Korea, Pakistan, or Iraq depends more on having reliable satellites or spies than on vast flows of electronic mail.

The information revolution alters patterns of complex interdependence by exponentially increasing the number of channels of communication in world politics—between individuals in networks, not just individuals within bureaucracies. But it exists in the context of an existing political structure, and its effects on the flows of different types of information vary vastly. Free information will flow faster without regulation. Strategic information will be protected as much as possible—for example, by encryption technologies. The flow of commercial information will depend on whether property rights are established in cyberspace. Politics will shape the information revolution as much as vice versa.

THE NATURE OF POWER

KNOWLEDGE IS power, but what is power? A basic distinction can be drawn between behavioral power—the ability to obtain outcomes you want—and resource power—the possession of resources that are usually associated with the ability to reach outcomes you want. Behavioral power, in turn, can be divided into hard and soft power. Hard power is the ability to get others to do what they otherwise would not do through threats or rewards. Whether by economic carrots or military sticks, the ability to coax or coerce has long been the central element of power. As we pointed out two decades ago, the ability of the less vulnerable to manipulate or escape the constraints of an interdependent relationship at low cost is an important source of power. For example, in 1971 the United States halted the convertibility of dollars into gold and increased its influence over the international monetary system. In 1973, Arab states temporarily gained power from an oil embargo.

Soft power, on the other hand, is the ability to get desired outcomes because others want what you want. It is the ability to achieve goals through attraction rather than coercion. It works by convincing others to follow or getting them to agree to norms and institutions that produce the desired behavior. Soft power can rest on the appeal of one's ideas or culture or the ability to set the agenda through standards and institutions that shape the preferences of others. It depends largely on the persuasiveness of the free information that an actor seeks to transmit. If a state can make its power legitimate in the eyes of others and establish international institutions that encourage others to define their interests in compatible ways, it may not need to expend as many costly traditional economic or military resources.

Hard and soft power are related, but they are not the same. The political scientist Samuel P. Huntington is correct when he says that material success makes a culture and ideology attractive, and that economic and military failure lead to self-doubt and crises of identity. He is wrong, however, when he argues that soft power rests solely on a foundation of hard power. The soft power of the Vatican did not wane because the size of the papal states diminished. Canada, Sweden, and the Netherlands have more influence than some other states with equivalent economic or military capabilities. The Soviet Union had considerable soft power in Europe after World War II but squandered it by invading Hungary and Czechoslovakia even when Soviet economic and military power continued to grow. Soft power varies over time and different domains. America's popular culture, with its libertarian and egalitarian currents, dominates film, television, and electronic communications. Not all aspects of that culture are attractive to everyone, for example conservative Muslims. Nonetheless, the spread of information and American popular culture has generally increased global awareness of and openness to American ideas and values. To some extent this reflects deliberate policies, but more often soft power is an inadvertent byproduct.

The information revolution is also affecting power measured in terms of resources rather than behavior. In the eighteenth-century European balance of power, territory, population, and agriculture provided the basis for infantry, and France was a principal beneficiary. In the nineteenth century, industrial capacity provided the resources that enabled Britain and, later, Germany to gain dominance. By the mid-twentieth century, science and particularly nuclear physics contributed crucial power resources to the United States and the Soviet Union. In the next century, information technology, broadly defined, is likely to be the most important power resource.

THE SMALL VERSUS THE LARGE

THE NEW conventional wisdom is that the information revolution has a leveling effect. As it reduces costs, economies of scale, and barriers of entry to markets, it should reduce the power of large states and enhance the power of small states and nonstate actors. In practice, however, international relations are more complex than the technological determinism this view suggests. Some aspects of the information revolution help the small, but some help the already large and powerful. There are several reasons.

First, important barriers to entry and economies of scale remain in some information-related aspects of power. For example, soft power is strongly affected by the cultural content of movies and television programs. Large, established entertainment industries often enjoy considerable economies of scale in content production and distribution.

The dominant American market share in films and television programs in world markets is therefore likely to continue.

Second, even where it is now cheap to disseminate existing information, the collection and production of new information often requires costly investments. In many competitive situations, the newness of information at the margin counts more than the average cost of all information. Intelligence is a good example. States like the United States, Britain, and France have capabilities for collecting intelligence that dwarf those of other nations. In some commercial situations, a fast follower can do better than a first mover, but in terms of power among states, it is usually better to be first.

Third, first movers are often the creators of the standards and architecture of information systems. The use of the English language and the pattern of top-level domain names on the Internet is a case in point. Partly because of the transformation of the American economy in the 1980s and partly because of large investments driven by the Cold War military competition, the United States was often first on the scene and still enjoys a lead in the application of a wide variety of information technologies.

Fourth, military power remains important in some critical domains of international relations. Information technology has some effects on the use of force that benefit the small and some that favor the powerful. The off-the-shelf commercial availability of what used to be costly military technologies benefits small states and nonstate actors and increases the vulnerability of large states. Information systems add lucrative targets for terrorist groups. Other trends, however, strengthen the already powerful. Many military analysts refer to a "revolution in military affairs" caused by the application of information technology. Space-based sensors, direct broadcasting, high-speed computers, and complex software provide the ability to gather, sort, process, transfer, and disseminate information about complex events that occur over a wide geographic area. This dominant battlespace awareness combined with precision force produces a powerful advantage. As the Gulf War showed, traditional assessments of balances of weapons platforms such as tanks or planes become irrelevant unless they include the ability to integrate information with those weapons. Many of the relevant technologies are available in commercial markets, and weaker states can be expected to have many of them. The key, however, will not be possession of fancy hardware or advanced systems but the ability to integrate a system of systems. In this dimension, the United States is likely to keep its lead. In information warfare, a small edge makes all the difference. Contrary to the expectations of some theorists, the information revolution has not greatly decentralized or equalized power among states. If anything, it has had the opposite effect.

THE POLITICS OF CREDIBILITY

WHAT ABOUT reducing the role of governments and the power of all states? Here the changes are more likely to be along the lines the modernists predicted. But to understand the effect of free information on power, one must first understand the paradox of plenty. A plenitude of information leads to a poverty of attention. Attention becomes the scarce resource, and those who can distinguish valuable signals from white noise gain power. Editors, filters, interpreters, and cue-givers become more in demand, and this is a source of power. There will be an imperfect market for evaluators. Brand names and the ability to bestow an international seal of approval will become more important.

But power does not necessarily flow to those who can withhold information. Under some circumstances private information can cripple the credibility of those who have it. For instance, economists point out that sellers of used cars know more about their defects than potential buyers. Moreover, owners of bad cars are more likely to sell than owners of good ones. Thus potential buyers discount the price they are willing to pay to adjust for unknown defects. Hence the superior information of sellers does not improve the average price they receive, but instead makes them unable to sell good used cars for their real value. Unlike asymmetrical interdependence in trade, where power goes to those who can afford to hold back or break trade ties, information power flows to those who can edit and credibly validate information to sort out what is both correct and important.

Hence, among editors and cue-givers, credibility is the crucial resource, and asymmetrical credibility is a key source of power. Establishing credibility means developing a reputation for providing correct information, even when it may reflect badly on the information provider's own country. The BBC, for example, has earned a reputation for credibility, while state-controlled radio stations in Baghdad, Beijing, and Havana have not. Reputation has always mattered in world politics, and it has become even more important because of the paradox of plenty. The low cost of transmitting data means that the ability to transmit it is much less important than it used to be, but the ability to filter information is more so. Political struggles focus less on control over the ability to transmit information than over the creation and destruction of credibility.

Three types of state action illustrate the value of credibility. Much of the traditional conduct of foreign policy occurs through the exchange of promises, which can be valuable only insofar as they are credible. Hence, governments that can credibly assure potential partners that they will not act opportunistically will gain advantages over competitors whose promises are less credible. During the Cold War, for example, the United States was a more credible ally for Western European countries than the Soviet Union because as a democracy the United States could more credibly promise not to seek to exploit or dominate its allies. Second, to borrow from capital markets at competitive interests rates requires credible information about one's financial situation. Finally, the exercise of soft power requires credibility in order to be persuasive. For instance, as long as the United States condoned racial segregation it could not be a credible advocate of universal human rights. But in June 1998, President Clinton could preach human rights to the Chinese—and in answer to a question at Beijing University about American shortcomings, could frankly admit that the United States needed to make further progress to realize its ideal of equality.

One implication of the abundance of free information sources and the role of credibility is that soft power is likely to become less a function of material resources. Hard power may be necessary—for instance, using force to take over a radio station—to generate soft power. Propaganda as a form of free information is not new. Hitler and Stalin used it effectively in the 1930s. Slobodan Milošević's control of television was crucial to his power in Serbia. In Moscow in 1993, a battle for power was fought at a TV station. In Rwanda, Hutu-controlled radio stations encouraged genocide. The power of broadcasting persists but will be increasingly supplemented by the Internet, with its multiple channels of communication controlled by multiple actors who cannot control one another by force. The issue is not only which actors own television networks, radio stations, or web sites—once a plethora of such sources exist—but who pays attention to which fountains of information and misinformation.

The shift from broadcasting to narrowcasting has major political implications.

In the case of worldwide television, wealth can also lead to soft power. For instance, CNN was based in Atlanta rather than Amman or Cairo because of America's leading position in the industry and technology. When Iraq invaded Kuwait in 1990, the fact that CNN was an American company helped to frame the issue, worldwide, as aggression. Had an Arab company been the world's dominant TV channel, perhaps the issue would have been framed as a justified attempt to reverse colonial humiliation.

Broadcasting is a type of free information that has long had an impact on public opinion. By focusing on certain conflicts and human rights problems, broadcasters have pressed politicians to respond to some foreign conflicts rather than others—say Somalia rather than southern Sudan. Not surprisingly, governments have sought to manipulate television and radio stations and have met with considerable success, since a relatively small number of broadcasting sites have been used to reach many people with the same message. However, the shift from broadcasting to narrowcasting has major political implications. Cable television and the Internet enable senders to segment and target audiences. Even more important politically, the Internet not only focuses attention but helps coordinate action across borders. Interactivity at low cost allows for the development of new virtual communities: people who imagine themselves as part of a single group regardless of how far apart they are physically from one another.

These technologies create new opportunities for NGOs. Advocacy networks' potential impact is vastly expanded by the information revolution, since the fax machine and the Internet enable them to send messages from the rain forests of Brazil or the sweatshops of

Southeast Asia. The recent Landmine Conference resulted from the activities of a coalition of network organizations working with middle-power governments like Canada, individual politicians like Senator Patrick Leahy (D-Vt.), and celebrities like Princess Diana to capture attention, set the agenda, and put pressure on political leaders. The role of NGOS was also an important channel of communication across delegations in the global warming discussions at Kyoto in December 1997. Environmental groups and industry competed in Kyoto for the attention of the media from major countries, basing their arguments in part on the findings of nongovernmental scientists.

There are substantial opportunities for a flowering of issue advocacy networks and virtual communities, but the credibility of these networks is fragile. Greenpeace, for instance, imposed large costs on Royal Dutch Shell by criticizing its planned disposal of its Brentspar drilling rig in the North Sea, but Greenpeace itself lost credibility when it later had to admit the inaccuracy of some of its claims. Atmospheric scientists' findings about climate change have gained credibility, not just from the prestige of science but from the procedures developed in the Intergovernmental Panel on Climate Change for extensive and careful peer review of scientific papers and intergovernmental vetting of executive summaries. The IPCC is an example of an information-legitimating institution whose major function is to give coherence and credibility to masses of scientific information about climate change.

As the IPCC example shows, the significance of credibility is giving increasing importance to transnational networks of like-minded experts. By framing issues where knowledge is important, such professional communities become important actors in forming coalitions and in bargaining processes. By creating knowledge, they can provide the basis for effective cooperation. But to be effective, the procedures by which this information is produced must appear unbiased. Scientific information is increasingly recognized as in part socially constructed. To be credible, the information must be produced through a process that is in accordance with professional norms and characterized by transparency and procedural fairness.

THE DEMOCRATIC ADVANTAGE

NOT ALL democracies are leaders in the information revolution, but many are. This is no accident. Their societies are familiar with the free exchange of information, and their institutions of governance are not threatened by it. They can shape information because they can also take it. Authoritarian states, typically among the laggards, have more trouble. Governments such as China's can still limit their citizens' access to the Internet by controlling service providers and monitoring the relatively small number of users. Singapore has thus far been able to reconcile its political controls with an increasing role for the Internet. But as societies like Singapore reach higher levels of development where more citizens want fewer restrictions on access to the Internet, Singapore runs the risk of losing the people who are its key resource for competing in the information economy. Thus Singapore is wrestling with the dilemma of reshaping its educational system to encourage the individual creativity that the information economy will demand while maintaining social controls over the flow of information.

Another reason that closed systems have become more costly is that it is risky for foreigners to invest funds in a country where the key decisions are made in an opaque fashion. Transparency is becoming a key asset for countries seeking investments. The ability to hoard information, which once seemed so valuable to authoritarian states, undermines the credibility and transparency necessary to attract investment on globally competitive terms. Geographical communities still matter most, but governments that want rapid development will have to give up some of the barriers to information flows that protected officials from outside scrutiny. No longer will governments that want high levels of development be able to afford the luxury of keeping their financial and political situations a secret.

From a business standpoint, the information revolution has vastly increased the marketability and value of commercial information by reducing costs of transmission and the transaction costs of charging information users. As Adam Smith would have recognized, the value of information increases when the costs of transmitting it decline, just as the value of a good increases when transportation costs fall, increasing demand by giving its makers a larger market. Politically, however, the most important shift has concerned free information. The ability to disseminate free information increases the potential for persuasion in world politics. NGOS and states can more readily influence the beliefs of people in other jurisdictions. If one actor can persuade others to adopt similar values and policies, whether it possesses hard power and strategic information may become less important. Soft power and free information can, if sufficiently persuasive, change perceptions of self-interest and thereby alter how hard power and strategic information are used. If governments or NGOS are to take advantage of the information revolution, they will have to establish reputations for credibility amid the white noise of the information revolution.

Cheap flows of information have enormously expanded the number and depth of transnational channels of contact. Nongovernmental actors have much greater opportunities to organize and propagate their views. States are more easily penetrated and less like black boxes. As a result, political leaders will find it more difficult to maintain a coherent ordering of foreign policy issues. Yet states are resilient, and some countries, especially large ones with democratic societies, are well-placed to benefit from an information society. Although the coherence of government policies may diminish in these pluralistic and penetrated states, their institutions will be attractive and their pronouncements will be credible. They will therefore be able to wield soft power to achieve many of their objectives. The future lies neither exclusively with the state nor with transnational relations: geographically based states will continue to structure politics in an information age, but they will rely less on material resources and more on their ability to remain credible to a public with increasingly diverse sources of information.

Refocusing the IMF

Martin Feldstein

OVERDOING IT IN EAST ASIA

IN THE Asian currency crisis, the International Monetary Fund is risking its effectiveness by the way it now defines its role as well as by its handling of the problems of the affected countries. The IMF's recent emphasis on imposing major structural and institutional reforms as opposed to focusing on balance-of-payments adjustments will have adverse consequences in both the short term and the more distant future. The IMF should stick to its traditional task of helping countries cope with temporary shortages of foreign exchange and with more sustained trade deficits.

Today's emphasis on structural and institutional reforms has not always been part of IMF programs. The IMF was founded in 1945 to help operate a system of fixed exchange rates, in which all currencies were pegged to the dollar, in turn fixed with respect to gold, that experts then considered necessary to encourage international trade. Although that system succeeded temporarily, differences in inflation between countries forced many to alter their currency values. When the fixed-rate system collapsed completely in 1971, the IMF was forced to find a new raison d'être.

The fund found a new and important role, which is still appropriate for the current crisis, in the 1980s. Changes in economic conditions led Mexico and other Latin American countries to announce they could not meet the interest and principal payments on their large borrowings from overseas commercial banks. A default on those obligations would have wiped out the capital of many leading banks in the United States,

---

MARTIN FELDSTEIN is Professor of Economics at Harvard University and President of the National Bureau of Economic Research.

Europe, and Japan, so the U.S. government provided a temporary bridge loan that allowed Mexico to meet its imminent payments. Negotiations then began between the Mexican government and representatives of the lending banks, who agreed to restructure the debts, lengthening maturities and lending additional money with which the borrowers could meet part of their interest obligations. Similar negotiations were later conducted with the other Latin American debtors.

To meet their interest obligations and reduce their outstanding debt, Latin American countries had to earn more foreign exchange by increasing their exports or decreasing their imports. So Latin American governments raised taxes, cut government outlays, and tightened credit to reduce domestic uses of national output. The IMF monitored these adjustments and provided moderate amounts of credit to indicate that it was satisfied with the policy progress that the debtors were making. But the primary provision of credit was left to negotiations between the foreign banks and each of the debtor countries.

Over time the process was successful. The region's economic growth eventually resumed, and the countries were generally able to service their rescheduled debts. The commercial banks wrote off some loans of small, heavily indebted countries. In the end the banks swapped their remaining loan balances for so-called Brady Bonds that had government guarantees but paid less interest or had a reduced principal. This approach succeeded because of a general recognition that the problem of the major Latin American countries was one of liquidity rather than insolvency—that is, they were temporarily unable to pay current foreign obligations but were not permanently unable to earn enough foreign currency by exporting to service and repay their debts.

The next major chapter in the IMF's history began with the collapse of the Soviet Union and the liberation of its former European satellites. These countries needed to shift from communism to a market economy and to integrate themselves into international financial markets. Their officials, bankers, and economists had little or no experience with market economics. The IMF could therefore provide useful advice on a much wider range of economic issues than it had previously done in Latin America or elsewhere in the world. Much of this advice—about the strategy of privatization, banking systems, and tax structures—

was useful. Much of it was also controversial. But while economists outside the fund had a variety of views about the right way for Russia and the other countries of Eastern Europe and the former Soviet Union to proceed, the IMF was generally able to get its way because it brought substantial financial rewards to countries that accepted its advice.

The IMF is now acting in Southeast Asia and Korea in much the same way that it did in Eastern Europe and the former Soviet Union: insisting on fundamental changes in economic and institutional structures as a condition for receiving IMF funds. It is doing so even though the situations of the Asian countries are very different from that of the former Soviet Union and Eastern Europe. In addition, the IMF is applying its traditional mix of fiscal policies (higher taxes, less government spending) and credit tightening (implying higher interest rates) that were successful in Latin America. To assess the appropriateness of these policies, it is necessary to understand what is happening in Asia.

THE ASIAN MELTDOWN

THE SOUTHEAST Asian currency collapse that began in Thailand was an inevitable consequence of persistent large current account deficits and of the misguided attempt of Thailand, Indonesia, Malaysia, and the Philippines to maintain fixed exchange rates relative to the dollar. Thailand's current account deficit—the sum of its trade deficit and the interest on its foreign obligations—had exceeded four percent of Thailand's GDP since 1990, implying that Thailand had to attract that much foreign capital each year. Such large current account deficits have inevitably ended in a sharp decline in the local currency's value when foreign creditors and domestic investors became concerned that the borrower would be unable to service its debts. Thailand's large current account deficit persisted for a surprisingly long time because creditors believed that Thailand might be "different" since much of the capital inflow came as direct investment by Japanese manufacturing firms and lending by their affiliated banks. Creditors also derived confidence from Thailand's high savings rate and its government budget surplus, noting that the current account deficit reflected enormously high business investment rather than government or consumer profligacy. But the primary thing that kept foreign funds coming to Thailand and local funds staying there was the combination of relatively high interest rates on Thai baht deposits and a promise that the baht's value would remain fixed at 25 baht per dollar. It looked like too good a deal to pass up.

But the baht's fixed value relative to the dollar could not be sustained. The pressure for a devaluation of the baht increased in 1996 and 1997 when the Japanese yen declined by 35 percent relative to the dollar. Since Japan is Thailand's major trading partner, the sharp rise in the value of the dollar (and therefore of the baht) relative to the yen made Thai products more expensive and therefore less competitive and pointed to even larger trade deficits in the future. Foreign speculators as well as local investors began to sell bahts. The Thai government secretly bought the baht to support its value but eventually had to give up. At that point the IMF stepped in with a multibillion dollar rescue plan.

The Thai currency collapse spread to Indonesia, Malaysia, and the Philippines as financial investors became worried about their large current account deficits, high ratios of foreign debt to local GDP, and deteriorating trade competitiveness. Each country was forced to abandon its fixed exchange-rate policy and let the market determine the currency's value. Indonesia lacked the reserves to meet its short-term obligations and called in the IMF. Malaysia has not yet done so, while the Philippines was already in an IMF program when the crisis began.

All of these countries clearly need to shrink their current account deficits by increasing exports and reducing imports. That in turn requires reductions in public and private consumption and investment. The proper remedy is a variant of the traditional IMF medicine tailored specifically to each country—some combination of reduced government spending, higher taxes, and tighter credit. Even in those countries where government budgets are already in surplus, an increase in taxes or a reduction in government spending will shrink the current account deficit. The experience in Latin America provides a useful model of what can be done.

But the IMF's role in Thailand and Indonesia went far beyond the role that it played in Latin America. Instead of relying on private banks and serving primarily as a monitor of performance, the IMF took the lead in providing credit. In exchange, it has imposed programs requiring governments to reform their financial institutions and to make substantial changes in their economic structures and political behavior. The conditions imposed on Thailand and Indonesia were more like the comprehensive reforms imposed on Russia, including the recent emphasis on reducing Russian corruption, than like the macroeconomic changes that were required in Latin America. In Indonesia, for example, in exchange for a $40 billion package (more than 25 percent of Indonesia's GDP), the IMF has insisted on a long list of reforms, specifying in minute detail such things as the price of gasoline and the manner of selling plywood. The government has also been told to end the country's widespread corruption and curtail the special business privileges used to enrich President Suharto's family and the political allies that maintain his regime. Although such changes may be desirable in many ways, past experience suggests that they are not needed to maintain a flow of foreign funds.

In Indonesia the IMF's reforms have specified minute details like the price of gasoline.

The Korean situation is different from that of the four countries of the Association of Southeast Asian Nations and is more important because its economy is the 11th-largest in the world. Korea's problem did not stem from an overvalued exchange rate and an excessive current account deficit. The value of the Korean won had not been fixed in recent years but had gradually adjusted to maintain Korea's competitiveness. A collapse of the market for semiconductors, a major Korean export, had caused Korea's current account deficit to jump from 1.7 percent of GDP in 1995 to 4.7 percent of GDP in 1996. But by mid-1997 it was already back to a 2.5 percent annual rate and heading lower.

The Korean economy was performing well: real GDP grew at eight percent per year in the 1990s, as it had in the 1980s, inflation was below five percent, and the unemployment rate was less than three percent. Although there were recent bankruptcies among the smaller business conglomerates and merchant banks, this was clearly an economy to envy. Korea got in trouble in mid-1997 because its business and financial institutions had incurred short-term foreign debts that far exceeded Korea's foreign exchange assets.

By October, U.S. commercial banks estimated that Korea's short-term debts were $110 billion—more than three times Korea's foreign exchange reserves. With investors nervous about emerging markets in general and Asia in particular, it is not surprising that the Korean won came under attack.

Since Korea's total foreign debt was only about 30 percent of GDP (among the lowest of all developing nations), this was clearly a case of temporary illiquidity rather than fundamental insolvency. Moreover, since the current account deficit was very small and rapidly shrinking, there was no need for the traditional IMF policy of reduced government spending, higher taxes, and tight credit. Yet something needed to be done to stop the loss of foreign exchange and to maintain bank lending to the country and its healthy businesses. Because of the overhang of excess short-term foreign liabilities, each foreign bank acting independently had a strong incentive not to roll over its loans. Investors, fearing a drain on Korea's reserves and a depressed won, were induced to anticipate the process by selling the won immediately.

What Korea needed was coordinated action by creditor banks to restructure its short-term debts, lengthening their maturity and providing additional temporary credits to help meet the interest obligations. The creditors should have preferred this course to having the borrowers default on their loans, just as the creditors did 15 years earlier in their negotiations with the Latin American debtors. The rate of interest required to attract such long-term foreign lending on a voluntary basis—and thereby avoid a withdrawal of private lending to other emerging-market countries—was about four percentage points above the interest rate on U.S. Treasury bonds and therefore well within what Korea could finance by its exports. During November the interest rate on ten-year dollar bonds issued by the government-backed Korea Development Bank varied between two percent and four percent above the interest rate on U.S. Treasury bonds. Even a four percent premium on a completely restructured Korean foreign debt would have been equal to only about one percent of Korea's GDP and about four percent of its exports. The IMF could have helped by providing a temporary bridge loan and then organizing the banks into a negotiating group. (In fact, the IMF did just that in late December with the help of the national central banks after its original plan had failed.)

Instead, the IMF organized a pool of $57 billion from official sources—the IMF, the World Bank, the U.S. and Japanese governments, and others—to lend to Korea so that its private corporate borrowers could meet their foreign currency obligations to U.S., Japanese, and European banks. In exchange for those funds, the IMF demanded a fundamental overhaul of the Korean economy and a contractionary macroeconomic policy of higher taxes, reduced spending, and high interest rates.

The IMF's program emphasized eight structural problems of the Korean economy that it said had to be changed. Foreign investors are not able to acquire Korean businesses by purchasing their shares or to own majority stakes in Korean businesses. Korea's domestic financial markets are not fully open to foreign banks and insurance companies. Imports of some industrial products are still restricted, especially Japanese cars. Korean banks do not apply good Western banking standards of credit evaluation but follow what might be called the Japanese development model, in which the government guides banks to lend to favored industries in exchange for an implicit guarantee of the loans. The Bank of Korea is not independent and does not have price stability as its only goal. The corporate structure involves large conglomerates (the *chaebols*) with an extremely wide range of activities and opaque financial accounts. Korean corporations generally have very high debt-to-capital ratios that make them risky debtors for domestic and foreign lenders. Finally, Korean labor laws make layoffs very difficult and provide strong impediments to the flow of workers between firms.

The IMF said that it would provide credit only as Korea altered these central features of its economy. It predicted that economic growth in 1998 would be only half the 1997 level and that the unemployment rate would double. These conditions would be exacerbated by the IMF's requirement for high interest rates and for tighter fiscal policy to reduce the budget deficit between 1997 and 1998. Many private observers estimated that the adverse effects on output and employment would be substantially worse.

EVALUATING THE STRATEGY

THE FUNDAMENTAL issue is the appropriate role for an international agency and its technical staff in dealing with sovereign countries that come to it for assistance. It is important to remember that the IMF cannot initiate programs but develops a program for a member country only when that country seeks help. The country is then the IMF's client or patient, but not its ward. The legitimate political institutions of the country should determine the nation's economic structure and the nature of its institutions. A nation's desperate need for short-term financial help does not give the IMF the moral right to substitute its technical judgments for the outcomes of the nation's political process.

The IMF should provide the technical advice and the limited financial assistance necessary to deal with a funding crisis and to place a country in a situation that makes a relapse unlikely. It should not use the opportunity to impose other economic changes that, however helpful they may be, are not necessary to deal with the balance-of-payments problem and are the proper responsibility of the country's own political system.

In deciding whether to insist on any particular reform, the IMF should ask three questions: Is this reform really needed to restore the country's access to international capital markets? Is this a technical matter that does not interfere unnecessarily with the proper jurisdiction of a sovereign government? If the policies to be changed are also practiced in the major industrial economies of Europe, would the IMF think it appropriate to force similar changes in those countries if they were subject to a fund program? The IMF is justified in requiring a change in a client country's national policy only if the answer to all three questions is yes.

The Korean case illustrates the need for this test very well. Although many of the structural reforms that the IMF included in its early-December program for Korea would probably improve the long-term performance of the Korean economy, they are not needed for Korea to gain access to capital markets. They are also among the most politically sensitive issues: labor market rules, regulations of corporate structure and governance, government-business relations, and international trade. The specific policies that the IMF insists must be changed are not so different from those in the major countries of Europe: labor market rules that cause 12 percent unemployment, corporate ownership structures that give banks and governments controlling interests in industrial companies, state subsidies to inefficient and loss-making industries, and trade barriers that restrict Japanese auto imports to a trickle and block foreign purchases of industrial companies.

Korea does not need structural reforms to gain immediate access to capital markets.

Imposing detailed economic prescriptions on legitimate governments would remain questionable even if economists were unanimous about the best way to reform the countries' economic policies. In practice, however, there are substantial disagreements about what should be done. Even when there has been near unanimity about the appropriate economic policies, the consensus has changed radically. After all, the IMF was created to defend and manage a fixed exchange-rate system that is now regarded as economically inappropriate and practically unworkable. Similarly, for a long time the advice to developing countries that came from the World Bank, the IMF's sister institution, and from leading academic specialists emphasized national plans for government-managed industrial development. The official and very influential U.N. Economic Commission for Latin America preached the virtues of protectionist policies to block industrial imports in order to encourage countries to develop their own manufacturing industries. Now the consensus of professional economists and international agencies calls for the opposite policies: flexible exchange rates, market-determined economic development, and free trade.

Today, there is nothing like unanimity about the appropriate policies for Korea or Southeast Asia. Korea's outstanding performance combining persistently high growth, low inflation, and low unemployment suggests that the current structure of the Korean economy may now be well suited to Korea's stage of economic and political development and to Korean cultural values stressing thrift, self-sacrifice, patriotism, and worker solidarity. Even if it were desirable for Korea to shift toward labor, goods, and capital markets more like those of the United States, it may be best to evolve in that direction more gradually and with fewer shocks to existing businesses. Unless the reforms could only be done under the duress of an IMF program or are specifically needed to end the liquidity problem, making the transition in the midst of a currency crisis would be very poor timing.

The short-term macroeconomic policies that the IMF prescribed for Korea are equally controversial. The program calls for the traditional IMF prescription of budget deficit reduction (by raising taxes and cutting government spending) and a tighter monetary policy (higher interest rates and less credit availability), which together depress growth and raise unemployment. But why should Korea be required to raise taxes and cut spending to lower its 1998 budget deficit when its national savings rate is already one of the highest in the world, when its 1998 budget deficit will rise temporarily because of the policy-induced recession, and when the combination of higher private savings and reduced business investment are already freeing up the resources needed to raise exports and shrink the current account deficit?

Under the IMF plan, the interest rate on won loans is now about 30 percent, while inflation is only 5 percent. Because of the high debt typical of most Korean companies, this enormously high real interest rate of 25 percent puts all of them at risk of bankruptcy. Why should Korea be forced to cause widespread bankruptcies by tightening credit when inflation is very low, when the rollover of bank loans and the demand for the won depend more on confidence than on Korean won interest rates, when the failures will reduce the prospect of loan repayment, and when a further fall in the won is an alternative to high interest rates as a way to attract won-denominated deposits? Although a falling won would increase the risk of bankruptcies among Korean companies with large dollar debts, the overall damage would be less extensive than the bankruptcies caused by very high won interest rates that would hurt every Korean company. Finally, why should Korea create a credit crunch that will cause even more corporate failures by enforcing the international capital standards for Korean banks when the Japanese government has just announced that it will not enforce those rules for Japanese banks in order to avoid a credit crunch in Japan?

ENCOURAGING EXCESSIVE RISK

THE IMF faces a serious dilemma whenever it deals with a country that cannot meet its obligation to foreign creditors. The IMF can encourage those creditors to roll over existing loans and provide new credit by promising them that they will be repaid in full. That type of guarantee was implicit in the IMF's $57 billion credit package for Korea. But promising creditors that they will not lose in the current crisis also encourages those lenders and others to take excessive future risks. Banks that expect loans to be guaranteed by governments do not look as carefully as they should at the underlying commercial credit risks. And when banks believe that the availability of dollars to meet foreign exchange obligations will be guaranteed by the IMF, they will not look carefully at the foreign exchange risk of the debtor countries.

There is no perfect solution to this "moral hazard" problem. In principle, the IMF and the Korean government should provide the guarantees needed to keep current creditors engaged while swearing that it is the last time that such guarantees will be provided. Although there may be no way to make such a promise persuasively, the IMF may have encouraged future lenders too much by the speed with which it took control—without waiting for lenders and borrowers to begin direct negotiations with each other. The call by IMF Managing Director Michel Camdessus for member governments to provide an additional $60 billion in IMF resources, on top of the $100 billion increase requested last September, just after announcing the Korean program in December also encourages banks and other lenders to believe they will be bailed out in the future.

At the same time, the message to emerging-market countries sent by painful and comprehensive reform programs was that they should avoid calling in the IMF. Malaysia is now doing just that, even though its conditions are roughly similar to those of Thailand and Indonesia. More generally, the tough program conditions make it difficult to get a country to work with the IMF until it is absolutely necessary. The IMF appears like the painful dentist of the old days: just as patients postponed visits until their teeth had to be pulled, the countries with problems wait too long to seek technical advice and modest amounts of financial help.

The desire to keep out of the IMF's hands will also cause emerging-market economies to accumulate large foreign currency reserves. A clear lesson of 1997 was that countries with large reserves could not be successfully attacked by financial markets. Hong Kong, Singapore, Taiwan, and China all have very large reserves, and all emerged relatively unscathed. A country can accumulate such reserves by running a trade surplus and saving the resulting foreign exchange. It would be unfortunate if developing countries that should be using their export earnings to finance imports of new plants and equipment use their scarce foreign exchange instead to accumulate financial assets.

Painful reforms can encourage countries to wait too long to seek modest financial help.

When the foreign exchange crisis hit Korea, the primary need was to persuade foreign creditors to continue to lend by rolling over existing loans as they came due. The key to achieving such credit without an IMF guarantee of outstanding loans was to persuade lenders that Korea's lack of adequate foreign exchange reserves was a temporary shortage, not permanent insolvency. By emphasizing the structural and institutional problems of the Korean economy, the fund's program and rhetoric gave the opposite impression. Lenders who listened to the IMF could not be blamed for concluding that Korea would be unable to service its debts unless its economy had a total overhaul. Given the magnitude of the prescribed changes, lenders might well be skeptical about whether Korea would actually deliver the required changes, regardless of what legislation it enacted. Even the $57 billion IMF pool did not promote confidence in Korea's ability to pay since the IMF emphasized that the money would be released only as Korea proved that it was conforming to the IMF program. Unsurprisingly, after the program was announced, the bond rating agencies downgraded Korean debt to junk bond status.

As a result, by late December Korea's reserves were almost gone, shrinking at a rate of $1 billion a day. The U.S. government and the IMF recognized that the original strategy had failed and agreed to accelerate $10 billion of the committed loans as a bridge to prevent a default. More important, the U.S. Federal Reserve and the other major central banks called in the leading commercial banks and urged them to create a coordinated program of short-term loan rollovers and longer-term debt restructuring. The banks agreed to roll over the loans coming due immediately, and the crisis was averted. The banks are now meeting with the Korean government to develop plans for longer-term restructuring. The situation in Korea might have been much better and the current deep crisis avoided had such negotiations begun much earlier.

Several features of the IMF plan are replays of the policies that Japan and the United States have long been trying to get Korea to adopt. These included accelerating the previously agreed upon reductions of trade barriers to specific Japanese products and opening capital markets so that foreign investors can have majority ownership of Korean firms, engage in hostile takeovers opposed by local management, and expand direct participation in banking and other financial services. Although greater competition from manufactured imports and more foreign ownership could in principle help the Korean economy, Koreans and others saw this aspect of the plan as an abuse of IMF power to force Korea at a time of weakness to accept trade and investment policies it had previously rejected.

The IMF would be more effective in its actions and more legitimate in the eyes of emerging-market countries if it pursued the less ambitious goal of maintaining countries' access to global capital markets and international bank lending. Its experts should focus on determining whether the troubled country's problem is one of short-term liquidity and, if so, should emphasize that in its advice and assistance. The IMF should eschew the temptation to use currency crises as an opportunity to force fundamental structural and institutional reforms on countries, however useful they may be in the long term, unless they are absolutely necessary to revive access to international funds. It should strongly resist the pressure from the United States, Japan, and other major countries to make their trade and investment agenda part of the IMF funding conditions.

The IMF should remember that the borrowers and the lending bankers or bondholders should bear primary responsibility for resolving the problems that arise when countries or their corporations cannot meet their international debt obligations. The IMF should provide technical assistance on how the debtors can improve their current account balances and increase their foreign exchange. It should act as a monitor of the success that the country is making in moving toward self-sustainable liquidity, providing its own funds as an indication of its confidence in the country's progress rather than as a bailout of international lenders and domestic borrowers. If the IMF can focus its attention on this narrower agenda, it can devote more of its scarce staff talent to the problem of crisis prevention. The IMF should work with countries that have not yet reached a currency crisis in order to prevent the large current account deficits or the excess short-term debts that could later precipitate a crisis. If the fund is seen more as a client-focused and supportive organization than as the imposer of painful contractions and radical economic reforms, it is likely to find that countries will be more willing to invite its assistance when it can be most helpful.

Response

In Defense of the IMF

Specialized Tools for a Specialized Task

Stanley Fischer

Martin Feldstein makes three criticisms of the International Monetary Fund's remedies for the Asian crisis ("Refocusing the IMF," March/April 1998). First, he argues that they are simply the same old IMF austerity medicine, inappropriately dispensed to countries suffering from a different malady. Second—and the main theme—he contends that by including in the program a number of structural elements, the IMF is unwisely going beyond its essential task of correcting the balance of payments and intruding into the countries' political processes. Third, he is troubled by the problem of moral hazard—the bailout issue.

In fact, the IMF-supported programs in Thailand, Indonesia, and South Korea are anything but the usual medicine, precisely because of their heavy structural components, which are included because structural problems lie at the heart of the economic crises in the three countries. To ignore the structural issues would invite a repetition of the crisis. The macroeconomic parts of these programs consist of a combination of tight money to restore confidence in the currency and a modest firming up of fiscal policy to offset in part the massive costs of financial restructuring. And the moral hazard concern, while essential to deal with, is easily exaggerated. Before turning to these issues, a brief discussion of the origins of the crisis is helpful.

CAUSES AND CONTAGION

The economic crisis in Asia unfolded against the backdrop of several decades of outstanding economic performance. Nevertheless, in 1996 some problems were becoming evident. First, Thailand and other countries were showing signs of overheating in the form of large trade deficits and real estate and stock market

STANLEY FISCHER is First Deputy Managing Director of the International Monetary Fund.

bubbles. Second, pegged exchange-rate regimes had been maintained for too long, encouraging heavy external borrowing, which led, in turn, to excessive foreign exchange risk exposure on the part of domestic financial institutions and corporations. Third, lax prudential rules and financial oversight had permitted the quality of banks' loan portfolios to deteriorate sharply.

Developments in the advanced economies and global financial markets also contributed to the unstable situation. Large private capital flows to emerging markets were driven in part by low interest rates in Japan and Europe, along with international investors' imprudent search for high yields. The appreciation of the dollar (to which local currencies were pegged) against the yen in mid-1995 was also important.

In Thailand, the crisis, if not its exact timing, was predicted. In the 18 months leading up to the floating of the Thai baht in July 1997, neither the IMF in its continuous dialogue with the Thai authorities nor increasing market pressure could overcome the government's reluctance to take action. Finally, in the absence of convincing policy action, and after Thailand had used up a large part of its reserves, the crisis broke out.

Should the IMF have gone public with its fears of a crisis? While the IMF knew that Thailand was extremely vulnerable, it could not predict with certainty whether, or when, a crisis would strike. For the IMF fire brigade to arrive with lights flashing and sirens wailing before a crisis occurs risks provoking a crisis that might not otherwise happen. That was not a risk that should have been taken.

Once the crisis hit Thailand, the contagion was relentless. Some of the infection reflected rational market behavior. The depreciation of the baht made Thai exports cheaper and therefore put downward pressure on neighbors' currencies. Moreover, after the Thai devaluation, investors took a closer look at Indonesia, South Korea, and neighboring countries and saw similar problems, particularly in the financial sector. Further, as currencies fell, residents rushed to buy foreign exchange to cover their dollar liabilities, intensifying exchange-rate pressures. But even if individual market participants behaved rationally, currencies depreciated far more than was required to correct their overvaluation. Put bluntly, markets overreacted.

Thailand, Indonesia, and South Korea faced a number of similar problems, including the loss of market confidence, deep currency depreciation, weak financial systems, and excessive unhedged foreign borrowing. All suffered from a lack of transparency about the ties between government, business, and banks. But when they requested IMF assistance, the countries also differed in the size of their current account deficits and the stages of crisis they were in. The design of the programs reflects these similarities and differences.

TOO TOUGH?

When they approached the IMF, Thailand and South Korea had perilously low reserves, and the Indonesian rupiah was excessively depreciated. The first order of business was to restore confidence in the currencies. To achieve this, countries have to make their currencies more attractive, which requires increasing interest rates temporarily—even if higher interest costs complicate the situation of weak banks and corporations. Once confidence is restored, interest rates can return to more normal levels.

Why not operate with lower interest rates and a greater devaluation? This is a relevant tradeoff, but there can be no question that the degree of devaluation of the Asian currencies from mid-1997 to the trough in early 1998 was excessive, for both the individual countries and the international system.

On the appropriate degree of fiscal tightening, the balance is a particularly fine one. At the onset of the crisis, countries needed to firm up their finances, both to cover the costs of financial restructuring, and—depending on the balance-of-payments situation—to reduce their current account deficits, which depend in part on the budget deficit. In calculating the fiscal tightening needed to offset financial restructuring costs, the programs included the expected interest costs—not the capital costs—to spread the costs of the adjustment over more time.

In Indonesia, the initial fiscal adjustment was one percent of GDP. In South Korea it was 1.5 percent of GDP. And in Thailand—reflecting its large current account deficit—it was 3 percent of GDP. After these initial adjustments, if the economic situation in a country weakens more than expected, as it has in these three Asian countries, the IMF has generally agreed to let the deficit widen and the stimulus of increased social spending and deficit expenditure take effect.

Thus in the macroeconomic picture, monetary policy had to be tight to restore confidence in the currency, and fiscal policy was tightened appropriately but not excessively at the start of each program, with automatic stabilizers subsequently allowed to work.

THE CENTRAL QUESTION

Feldstein proposes three questions the IMF should consider in deciding whether to include a particular measure in a program: whether it is needed to restore access to international capital markets, whether it is a technical measure that does not interfere unnecessarily with the jurisdiction of a sovereign government, and whether the IMF would ask for similar measures in major industrial countries. The IMF programs for the countries embroiled in the Asian crisis pass all three tests.

However, these three criteria omit the central question: Does the program address the underlying causes of the crisis? Financial sector and other structural reforms are vital to the reform programs of Thailand, Indonesia, and South Korea because the problems of weak financial institutions, inadequate bank regulation and supervision, and the complicated and non-transparent relations among governments, banks, and corporations were central to the economic crisis. IMF lending to these countries would serve no purpose if these problems were not addressed. Nor would it be in the countries' interest to leave the structural and governance issues aside: markets are skeptical of halfhearted reform efforts.

The charge that the IMF risks a moral hazard by coming to the assistance of countries in crisis has two parts: that officials in member countries may take excessive risks because they know the IMF will be there to bail them out, and that because the IMF will come to the rescue, investors do not appraise risks accurately and are too willing to lend. To think that policymakers pursue risky courses of action because they know the IMF safety net will catch them if things go badly is far-fetched. Countries try to avoid going to the fund; policymakers whose countries end up in trouble generally do not survive politically. In this regard, attaching conditions to assistance gives policymakers incentives to do the right thing. Indeed, these incentives have been evident in the preemptive reforms some countries have adopted.

The thornier issues arise on the side of investors. Most investors in the Asian crisis countries have taken heavy losses, including equity investors and many who lent to corporations and banks. By the end of 1997, foreign equity investors had lost nearly three-quarters of the value of their equity holdings in some Asian markets. Many Asian firms and financial institutions will, unfortunately, go bankrupt, and their foreign and domestic lenders will share the losses. Some short-term creditors, notably those involved in the interbank market, were protected for a while because the IMF sought to avert a formal debt moratorium for fear it would lead to a rapid withdrawal of funds from other countries. In the case of South Korea, the creditor banks have now been bailed *in,* and a similar process is getting under way in Indonesia. Further, earnings reports indicate that, overall, the crisis has been costly for foreign commercial banks.

None of this is to deny the existence of a moral hazard. Better ways of dealing with it must be found. But surely investors will not conclude that they need not worry about risks because the IMF will save them. Investors have been hit hard, as they should have been, for lending unwisely.

BRINGING BACK GROWTH

The alternative proposed by some critics is to leave it to countries and their creditors to sort out their debts. Given that the debts involved generally include both public and private obligations, and because everyone benefits whether or not they make the sacrifices necessary to help out, the experience—from the interwar period and the 1980s—is that such solutions have been protracted and that countries that have undertaken them have been denied market access for a long time at a significant cost to growth. By contrast, in the Mexican crisis of 1994-95, market access was regained in just a few months, and within a year Mexico, assisted by its ability to tap international capital markets, registered impressive growth. Similarly, South Korea has already returned to international markets, and Thailand will soon. The second reason that the IMF tried to help countries avoid a standstill was a fear of contagion. The IMF continues to believe that a standstill in one country, when markets were highly sensitive, would have spread to other countries and possibly other continents.

The basic approach of the IMF to these crises has been appropriate—not perfect, to be sure, but far better than if the structural elements had been ignored or the fund had not been involved. Of course, one cannot know for certain what would have happened had there been no official lending. But despite the instability in Indonesia, the crisis has been contained, and it is reasonable to believe that, deep and unfortunate as the crises in individual countries have been, growth in Korea and Thailand can resume by the end of the year.

The Capital Myth

The Difference between Trade in Widgets and Dollars

Jagdish Bhagwati

In the aftermath of the Asian financial crisis, the mainstream view that dominates policy circles, indeed the prevalent myth, is that despite the striking evidence of the inherently crisis-prone nature of freer capital movements, a world of full capital mobility continues to be inevitable and immensely desirable. Instead of maintaining careful restrictions, we are told, the only sensible course is to continue working toward unfettered capital flows; the favored solution is to turn the IMF even more firmly into an international lender of last resort that dispenses bailout funds to crisis-afflicted countries. The IMF took an important step in this direction at its annual meeting in Hong Kong last September, when the Interim Committee issued a statement virtually endorsing an eventual move to capital account convertibility—which means that you and I, nationals or foreigners, could take capital in and out freely, in any volume and at any time—for IMF members. The obligations originally listed in 1944 in the Articles of Agreement, on the other hand, included only "avoidance of restrictions on payments for current transactions" and did not embrace capital account convertibility as an obligation or even a goal.

This is a seductive idea: freeing up trade is good, why not also let capital move freely across borders? But the claims of enormous benefits from free capital mobility are not persuasive. Substantial gains have been asserted, not demonstrated, and most of the payoff can be obtained by direct equity investment. And even a richer IMF with attendant changes in its methods of operation will probably not rule out crises or reduce their costs significantly. The myth to the contrary has been created by what one might christen the Wall Street–Treasury complex, following in the footsteps of President Eisenhower, who had warned of the military-industrial complex.

CAPITAL MOBILITY IDEOLOGY

Until the Asian crisis sensitized the public to the reality that capital movements could repeatedly generate crises, many assumed that free capital mobility among

---

JAGDISH BHAGWATI is Arthur Lehman Professor of Economics at Columbia University. He was the Economic Policy Adviser to the Director-General of the General Agreement on Tariffs and Trade from 1991 to 1993.

all nations was exactly like free trade in their goods and services, a mutual-gain phenomenon. Hence restricted capital mobility, just like protectionism, was seen to be harmful to economic performance in each country, whether rich or poor. That the gains might be problematic because of the cost of crises was not considered.

However, the Asian crisis cannot be separated from the excessive borrowings of foreign short-term capital as Asian economies loosened up their capital account controls and enabled their banks and firms to borrow abroad. In 1996, total private capital inflows to Indonesia, Malaysia, South Korea, Thailand, and the Philippines were $93 billion, up from $41 billion in 1994. In 1997, that suddenly changed to an outflow of $12 billion. Hence it has become apparent that crises attendant on capital mobility cannot be ignored.

Although it is conceded that this downside exists, many claim that it can be ameliorated, if not eliminated, and that free capital mobility's immense advantages can be enjoyed by all. Conservatives would do this by letting the markets rip, untended by the IMF, which could then be sidelined or even disbanded. Liberals would do it instead by turning the IMF into the world's lender of last resort, dispensing funds during crises with several sorts of conditions, and overseeing, buttressing, and managing the world of free capital mobility.

To understand why neither of these modifications is enough, it is necessary to understand why the original version of the myth, which has steadily propelled the IMF into its complacent and dangerous moves toward the goal of capital account convertibility, was just that. True, economists properly say that there is a correspondence between free trade in goods and services and free capital mobility: interfering with either will produce efficiency losses. But only an untutored economist will argue that, therefore, free trade in widgets and life insurance policies is the same as free capital mobility. Capital flows are characterized, as the economic historian Charles Kindleberger of the Massachusetts Institute of Technology has famously noted, by panics and manias.

Each time a crisis related to capital inflows hits a country, it typically goes through the wringer. The debt crisis of the 1980s cost South America a decade of growth. The Mexicans, who were vastly overexposed through short-term inflows, were devastated in 1994. The Asian economies of Thailand, Indonesia, and South Korea, all heavily burdened with short-term debt, went into a tailspin nearly a year ago, drastically lowering their growth rates. Sure enough, serious economic downturns and crises can arise even when governments are not particularly vulnerable due to short-term borrowing: macroeconomic mismanagement in Japan has restrained its growth rate for nearly seven years now, and Japan is still a net lender of capital. But it is a non sequitur to suggest, as the defenders of free capital mobility do, that this possibility somehow negates the fact that short-term borrowings under free capital mobility will be, and have been, a source of considerable economic difficulty.

DOWNSIZING GAINS

When a crisis hits, the downside of free capital mobility arises. To ensure that capital returns, the country must do everything it can to restore the confidence of those who have taken their money out. This typically means raising interest rates, as the IMF has required of Indonesia. Across Asia this

ARCHIVE PHOTOS

Crisis on line one: Filipino traders react as Manila's stock market tumbles, October 28, 1997

has decimated firms with large amounts of debt. It also means having to sell domestic assets, which are greatly undervalued because of the credit crunch, in a fire sale to foreign buyers with better access to funds. (Economists have usually advised the exact opposite in such depressed circumstances: restricting foreign access to a country's assets when its credit, but not that of others, has dried up.) Thus, Thailand and South Korea have been forced to further open their capital markets, even though the short-term capital inflow played a principal role in their troubles in the first place.

Besides suffering these economic setbacks, these countries have lost the political independence to run their economic policies as they deem fit. That their independence is lost not directly to foreign nations but to an IMF increasingly extending its agenda, at the behest of the U.S. Congress, to invade domestic policies on matters of social policy—as with the 1994 Sanders-Frank Amendment, which seeks to attach labor standards conditions to any increase in bailout funds—is small consolation indeed.

Thus, any nation contemplating the embrace of free capital mobility must reckon with these costs and also consider the probability of running into a crisis. The gains from economic efficiency that would flow from free capital mobility, in a hypothetical crisis-free world, must be set against this loss if a wise decision is to be made.

None of the proponents of free capital mobility have estimated the size of the gains they expect to materialize, even leaving out the losses from crises that can ensue. For free trade, numerous studies have measured the costs of protection. The overwhelming majority of trade economists judge the gains from free trade to be significant, coming down somewhere between Paul Krugman's view that they are too small to be taken seriously and Jeffrey Sachs' view that they are huge and cannot be ignored. But all we have from the proponents of capital mobility is banner-waving, such as that of Bradford De Long, the Berkeley economist and former deputy assistant secretary for economic policy in the Clinton administration:

> So now we have all the benefits of free flows of international capital. These benefits are mammoth: the ability to borrow abroad kept the Reagan deficits from crushing U.S. growth like an egg, and the ability to borrow from abroad has enabled successful emerging market economies to double or triple the speed at which their productivity levels and living standards converge to the industrial core.

And of Roger C. Altman, the investment banker, who served in the Treasury Department under Presidents Clinton and Carter:

> The worldwide elimination of barriers to trade and capital . . . have created the global financial marketplace, which informed observers hailed for bringing private capital to the developing world, encouraging economic growth and democracy.[1]

These assertions assume that free capital mobility is enormously beneficial while simultaneously failing to evaluate its crisis-prone downside. But even a cursory glance at history suggests that these gains may be negligible. After all, China and Japan, different in politics and sociology as well as historical experience, have registered remarkable growth rates without capital account convertibility. Western Europe's return to prosperity was also achieved without capital account convertibility. Except for Switzerland, capital account liberalization was pretty slow at the outset and did not gain strength until the late 1980s, and some European countries, among them Portugal and Ireland, did not implement it until the early 1990s.

Besides, even if one believes that capital flows are greatly productive, there is still an important difference between embracing free portfolio capital mobility and having a policy of attracting direct equity investment. Maybe the amount of direct foreign investment that a country attracts will be reduced somewhat by not having freedom of portfolio capital flows, but there is little evidence for this assertion. Even then such a loss would be a small fraction of the gains from having a pro–foreign investment strategy.

A WALL STREET–TREASURY COMPLEX

That brings us to the myth that crises under capital account convertibility can be eliminated. We have, of course, heard this assertion before as each crisis has been confronted, and then we have been hit by yet another one. Like cats, crises have many lives, and macroeconomists, never a tribe that enjoyed a great reputation for getting things right or for agreeing among themselves, have been kept busy adding to the taxonomy of crises and their explanations. None of the solutions currently propounded can

[1]Bradford De Long, "What's Wrong with Our Bloody Economies?" January 11, 1998, from his World Wide Web page, http://econ161.berkeley.edu/; Roger C. Altman, "The Nuke of the 90's," *The New York Times Magazine*, March 1, 1998, p. 34.

really rid the system of free capital mobility of instability.

Thus, while no one can disagree with Secretary of the Treasury Robert Rubin's contention that reform of banking systems around the world will help, few should agree with him that it will eliminate the crises that unregulated capital flows inherently generate. Nor can the abolition of the IMF and its lender of last resort bailouts be the magic bullet: there were crises before the writer Walter Bagehot invented this function for domestic central banks in the nineteenth century. Nor can making the IMF more powerful kill the crises or give it the nonexistent macroeconomic wisdom to manage them at least cost when they arise.

In short, when we penetrate the fog of implausible assertions that surrounds the case for free capital mobility, we realize that the idea and the ideology of free trade and its benefits—and this extends to the continuing liberalization of trade in goods and financial and other services at the World Trade Organization—have, in effect, been hijacked by the proponents of capital mobility. They have been used to bamboozle us into celebrating the new world of trillions of dollars moving about daily in a borderless world, creating gigantic economic gains, rewarding virtue and punishing profligacy. The pretty face presented to us is, in fact, a mask that hides the warts and wrinkles underneath.

The question, then, is why the world has nonetheless been moving in this direction. The answer, as always, reflects ideology and interests—that is, lobbies. The ideology is clearly that of markets. The steady move away from central planning, overregulation, and general overreach in state intervention toward letting markets function has now reached across many sectors and countries. This is indeed all to the good and promises worldwide prosperity. But this wave has also lulled many economists and policymakers into complacency about the pitfalls that certain markets inherently pose even when they were understood in the classroom. Free capital mobility is just one example of this unwarranted attitude. Indeed, Stanley Fischer, the deputy managing director of the IMF, admitted in a February appearance on the *Charlie Rose* show on PBS that he had underestimated the probability of such crises arising in a world of capital mobility.

But interests have also played a central role. Wall Street's financial firms have obvious self-interest in a world of free capital mobility since it only enlarges the arena in which to make money. It is not surprising, therefore, that Wall Street has put its powerful oar into the turbulent waters of Washington political lobbying to steer in this direction. Thus, when testifying before the Senate Foreign Relations Committee on South Asia in March 1995, right after the Mexican peso crisis, I was witness to the grilling of Undersecretary of Commerce Jeffrey E. Garten on why India's financial system was not fully open to U.S. firms. To his credit, Garten said that this was not exactly a propitious time for the United States to pressure India in this direction.

Then again, Wall Street has exceptional clout with Washington for the simple reason that there is, in the sense of a power elite à la C. Wright Mills, a definite networking of like-minded luminaries among the powerful institutions—Wall Street, the Treasury Department, the State Department, the IMF, and the World Bank most prominent among them. Secretary Rubin comes from Wall Street; Altman went from Wall Street to the Treasury and back; Nicholas Brady, President Bush's Secretary of the Treasury, is back in finance as well; Ernest Stern, who has served as acting president of the World Bank, is now managing director of J.P. Morgan; James Wolfensohn, an investment banker, is now president of the World Bank. One could go on.

This powerful network, which may aptly, if loosely, be called the Wall Street–Treasury complex, is unable to look much beyond the interest of Wall Street, which it equates with the good of the world. Thus the IMF has been relentlessly propelled toward embracing the goal of capital account convertibility. The Mexican bailout of 1994 was presented as necessary, which was true. But so too was the flip side, that the Wall Street investors had to be bailed out as well, which was not. Surely other policy instruments, such as a surcharge, could have been deployed simultaneously to punish Wall Street for its mistakes. Even in the current Asian crisis, particularly in South Korea, U.S. banks could all have been forced to the bargaining table, absorbing far larger losses than they did, but they were cushioned by the IMF acting virtually as a lender of first, rather than last, resort.

And despite the evidence of the inherent risks of free capital flows, the Wall Street-Treasury complex is currently proceeding on the self-serving assumption that the ideal world is indeed one of free capital flows, with the IMF and its bailouts at the apex in a role that guarantees its survival and enhances its status. But the weight of evidence and the force of logic point in the opposite direction, toward restraints on capital flows. It is time to shift the burden of proof from those who oppose to those who favor liberated capital.

Globalization and Its Discontents

Navigating the Dangers of a Tangled World

Richard N. Haass and Robert E. Litan

The period immediately following the Second World War, which produced the Marshall Plan, NATO, and the U.S.-Japan security treaty, is rightly regarded as foreign policy's golden era. But it also saw the birth of comparably successful economic institutions—such as the International Monetary Fund, the World Bank, the General Agreement on Tariffs and Trade—designed to promote long-term prosperity through stable exchange rates, worldwide development, and open trade. Today these institutions are increasingly subject to criticism. The IMF, for instance, has come under attack for imposing drastic conditions in its "rescues" of Mexico in 1995 and Asia today. The World Trade Organization, formed in 1995 as the result of American calls for a body to resolve market-access disputes, has been attacked in this country for usurping America's sovereignty. And doubts abound about the role of development banks in an era of massive direct foreign investment.

The gap between the legacy of Bretton Woods and the economic and political demands of the modern world is growing. Much of this change is driven by rapid advances in, and thus lower costs of, communications, information flows, and travel. Official policy, much of it American, has played its part by reducing barriers to the movement of goods and capital across national boundaries. The result has been more intrusive and intense economic interaction—including the explosive growth of world capital markets, which led to the demise of fixed exchange rates—between a large and growing number of entities outside government control, a phenomenon that has come to be called "globalization."

But globalization has its problems. In some quarters it is seen as having caused the rapid flows of investment that moved in and out of countries as investor sentiment changed and were behind the Mexican and Asian financial crises. In the United

---

RICHARD N. HAASS, Director of the Program in Foreign Policy Studies at the Brookings Institution, is the author of *The Reluctant Sheriff: The United States after the Cold War*. ROBERT E. LITAN, Director of Brookings' Program in Economic Studies, is coauthor of *Globaphobia: Confronting Fears about Open Trade*.

[2]

States it is blamed for job losses, increasing income inequality, and stagnant or deteriorating real wages. Domestic discontent with globalization thwarted the passage last year of legislation that would have granted the president "fast track" authority to negotiate trade arrangements that Congress could not modify.

Globalization has become a target. Its dangers must be navigated successfully or the United States and others may be compelled to backtrack, diminishing the free movement of goods, services, and capital, which would result in slower growth, less technological innovation, and lower living standards.

FREE-MARKET FOREIGN POLICY?

In this new world, poor economic policymaking, corrupt banking practices, dishonest accounting, and unrealistic currency alignments can have an impact on societies far removed. Although the United States, with its vast internal market, is considerably less "globalized" than other industrialized countries, millions of American jobs and billions of dollars are tied to economic developments elsewhere.

If there is consensus on the diagnosis, there is none on the prescription. There are at least three fundamentally different approaches to addressing the problems of the global economy.

The first embraces the free market and would abandon IMF-like rescue packages. It is motivated by the belief that the IMF lulls governments, investors, and lenders into recklessness. Emboldened by the prospect that the IMF will come to their rescue, they are free to act irresponsibly. In the words of George Shultz, William Simon, and Walter Wriston, IMF "interference will only encourage more crises." Mexico, in this view, led to Asia.

The laissez-faire, free-market approach looks good in the abstract because markets reward sound investments and regulatory practices and punish poor ones. In principle, it can provide incentives for investors to avoid overly risky investments and for governments to adopt prudent policies. To international free marketeers, safety nets destroy this incentive.

But this critique goes too far. Governments submitting to IMF rescue plans must often agree to wrenching reforms—not the kind of experience that invites other governments to be reckless. Similarly, investors in equity markets in Mexico and Asia were hit by depressed local stock prices and heavily devalued local currencies. The only parties that emerged relatively unscathed, and thus for whom the free market critique has some relevance, were certain creditors: holders of Mexican government debt during the Mexican crisis and banks in the recent Asian crisis.

The solution to this problem is not to remove the IMF—the international lender of last resort—but to develop ways to warn banks and other creditors that they will suffer in the event of a future crisis. During the Depression, Americans learned the cost of not having a functioning lender of last resort: a wave of bank and corporate failures, aggravated by a shortage of liquidity that the Federal Reserve failed to provide. The international equivalent of having no Fed is standing idly by while currencies plummet, countries run out of foreign exchange, trade and investment come to a halt, and crises in one region spread to others.

A hands-off approach would risk transforming limited crises into something much more costly. More than economics is at stake. Years of punishment by the marketplace are simply not acceptable when immediate strategic interests are involved, as they are, for example, in Mexico or South Korea. For better or worse, the United States cannot afford the collapse of countries vital to its national interest.

GOVERNING GLOBALIZATION

The second approach to taming the dangers of globalization could hardly be more different. It suggests the creation of new institutions to lend structure and direction to the global marketplace, complementing what is seen as the constructive but inadequate roles of the IMF and other bodies. For example, George Soros, arguing that "international capital movements need to be supervised and the allocation of credit regulated," has recommended creating the international equivalent of the United States' Fannie Mae, which guarantees residential mortgages for a fee. He calls for the establishment of an "International Credit Insurance Corporation" that would guarantee private sector loans up to a specified amount for a modest charge, while requiring that the borrowers' home countries provide a complete financial picture in order for them to qualify.

Henry Kaufman, a Wall Street economist, would go even further, creating a "Board of Overseers of Major International Institutions and Markets" that would set minimum capital requirements for all institutions, establish uniform accounting and lending standards, and monitor performance. It would even discipline those who did not meet these criteria by limiting the ability of those who remained outside the system to lend, borrow, and sell.

Governments are sure to resist supranational bodies that so fundamentally challenge their sovereignty. Moreover, except for extreme crises when an IMF-like rescue is warranted, it is difficult to understand why international officials could determine how much credit to allocate better than the market. There is more than a little irony in applying the "Asian model" of centralization to the international economy just when the model has been so thoroughly discredited.

A third approach, which would leave the basic architecture of the international economy alone but still do some "remodeling," would involve a number of reforms designed to structure and discipline financial operations and transactions. This managed approach would eschew the heavy hand of international regulation but aim to maintain the element of risk essential to capitalism without removing the safety net provided by the IMF. This approach is closest to the manner in which the United States dealt with the savings and loan and banking crises of the 1980s: enacting legislation requiring shareholders to maintain a larger financial commitment to their banks while making it more difficult for regulators and policymakers to bail out large, uninsured depositors who could previously count on being protected. The challenge for the international community is to introduce the equivalent of the U.S. reforms at both the national and international levels.

Such reforms are already being worked on at the behest of the IMF. They include improving the supervision of financial institutions, instituting Western-style accounting practices in banks and corporations, and opening up markets to foreign investment. To ensure that these reforms are carried out, some other international body, such as the Bank for International Settlements or perhaps a nongovernmental organization, should issue regular "report cards" on individual countries' progress. In addition, the IMF must press countries to be forthcoming with accurate information about key financial data, including their current account positions, foreign exchange reserves, and short-term indebtedness to foreign creditors. Banks and investors will favor countries that are positively rated, and penalize or avoid those that are not. Governments and institutions will introduce desirable reforms lest they lose out.

More transparency and information is necessary but not sufficient for markets to avoid excesses. The challenge is to find effective ways of addressing the free market critique. A possible solution is for the IMF to condition its assistance on countries' penalizing all lenders of foreign currency in the event IMF intervention is required. In particular, the model legislation that each country could adopt would require (as long as an IMF rescue is in effect) that creditors automatically suffer some loss of their principal when their debt matures and is not rolled over or extended. This approach would discourage the sudden outflow of maturing debt when countries can least afford it. The threat of automatic loss in the event a country experiences economic crisis could underscore to banks and other creditors that their money is at risk and that they can no longer count on the IMF to bail them out. Creditors would respond, of course, by insisting on higher interest rates for borrowers with opaque or poorly capitalized balance sheets. But that is precisely the point: the price of loans should better reflect the risk of not getting repaid.

The Asian crisis demonstrates the need for more formal bankruptcy codes and mechanisms for restructuring the balance sheets of heavily indebted firms without necessarily shutting them down. Existing international institutions can assist countries in this area, as well as in strengthening bank supervision and accounting standards, but there is no need to establish a new international bankruptcy court or to vest existing international institutions with such powers. The United States has a bankruptcy code and process that handles insolvency of firms located here, even when they have foreign creditors. There is no reason why other countries cannot do the same thing.

THE HOME FRONT

To paraphrase former House Speaker Tip O'Neill, all economics is local. Policies promoting unfettered trade and investment will be rejected by Congress unless steps are taken to build a firm domestic political base. Once again, there are three approaches to choose from, running the gamut from laissez faire to heavy regulation. A pure market approach—one that would let the chips (and the workers) fall where they may—would be neither fair nor politically sustainable. Some sort of safety net is both desirable and necessary. At the same time, it would be foolish to try to insulate Americans from all of globalization's effects. It is impossible to protect jobs rendered obsolete by technological change and foreign competition. What lies between is a managed approach that helps workers cope with the consequences of globalization. It would both change and supplement existing programs and policies.

Since 1962, American policymakers have provided extended unemployment insurance to workers who can prove they were displaced primarily because of international trade. But this discourages workers from looking for employment, channeling them toward government training programs with little proven success. Moreover, it does not compensate workers for the cuts in pay they take even after finding new jobs. A more effective program would pay workers a portion of the difference between their wages at their previous and new jobs. This kind of earnings insurance would encourage workers to take new jobs even if they paid less, and offer the only real training that works—on the job. Workers could also be provided with benefits—health insurance, pensions, training, and unemployment insurance—that they could take with them when moving to a new employer.

Some will argue that portable benefits and earnings insurance are not enough. But globalization is a reality, not a choice. "You can run but you can't hide" might serve as the mantra for the age.

Those who urge us to hide by resurrecting barriers to trade and investment, with the ostensible aim of insulating Americans from the forces of globalization, would abandon America's commitment to the spread of markets and democracy around the world at precisely the moment these ideas are ascendant. Moreover, the potential economic and political cost would be enormous, depriving Americans of cheaper and in some cases higher quality goods and services, as well as denying them the opportunity to work at better paying jobs that depend on exports.

The real choice for governments is not how best to fight globalization but how to manage it, which will require creative policies both at home and abroad. It is ironic: the age of globalization may well be defined in part by challenges to the nation-state, but it is still states and governments—by the practices they adopt, the arrangements they enter into, and the safety nets they provide—that will determine whether we exploit or squander the potential of this era.